This Curriculum Covers:

- Reading
- Handwriting
- Creative Writing
- Spelling
- Classical Music
- Mathematics
- Science
- History
- Art, Drawing
- Library Skills
- Unit Studies
- Logic Games

MY NAME:

Age: Date:

By: Sarah Janisse Brown, Tolik Trishkin, Tanya Hulinska & Anastasia Fitas

We use the Dyslexie Font by Christian Boer

The Thinking Tree Publishing Company, LLC

FUNSCHOOLINGBOOKS.COM

Copyright 2016 ~ Do Not Copy

INSTRUCTIONS

LEARN ALL ABOUT ANIMALS!

DRAW FIVE THINGS

That you want to know about animals.

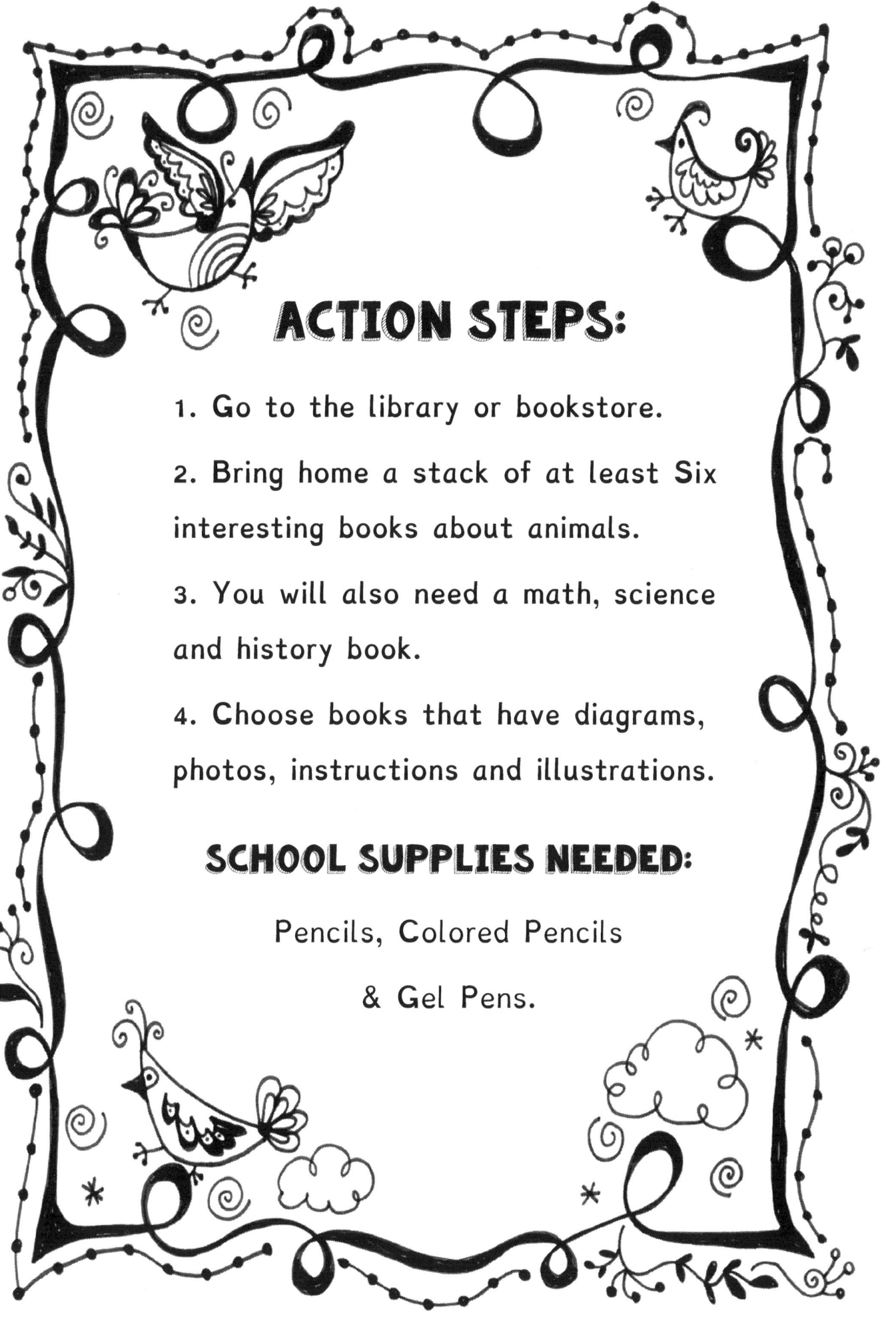

GO TO THE LIBRARY AND CHOOSE SIX BOOKS.

1. Write down the titles on each book cover below.

2. Keep your stack of books in a safe place so you can read a few pages from your books daily.

3. Ask your teacher how many pages to do each day in this Journal. Five to eight pages is normal for kids your age.

MY LIBRARY BOOKS:

MY HOMESCHOOLING CURRICULUM:

SCIENCE:

MATH:

HISTORY:

You may choose new books any time.
Flip to the back for more book pages.
Keep all your books in a basket
with your pens and pencils.

FIVE FACTS ABOUT ME:

1._____

2._____

3._____

4._____

5._____

NUMBER SEARCH!

Find each number between 1 and 100

Today's Date:

TO-DO LIST

1._____

2._____

3._____

4._____

Draw a Wild Animal

How are you FEELING TODAY?

Draw a Pet

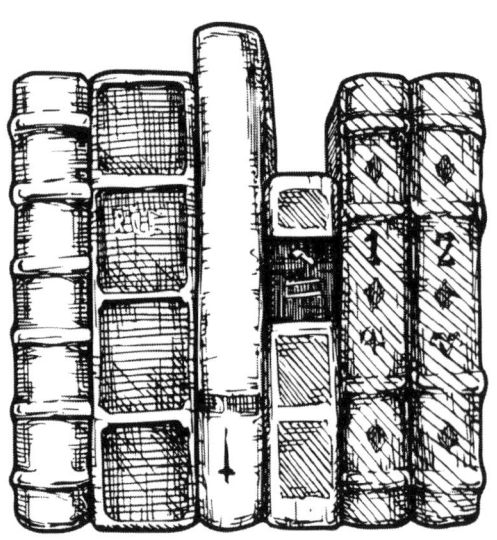

Ask your teacher to help you decide how many books to read from each day. #_____

Write and draw about what you are reading.

ORIGAMI CHALLENGE
CAN YOU MAKE THIS ANIMAL?

Set a timer.

Minutes:_____   Seconds:_____

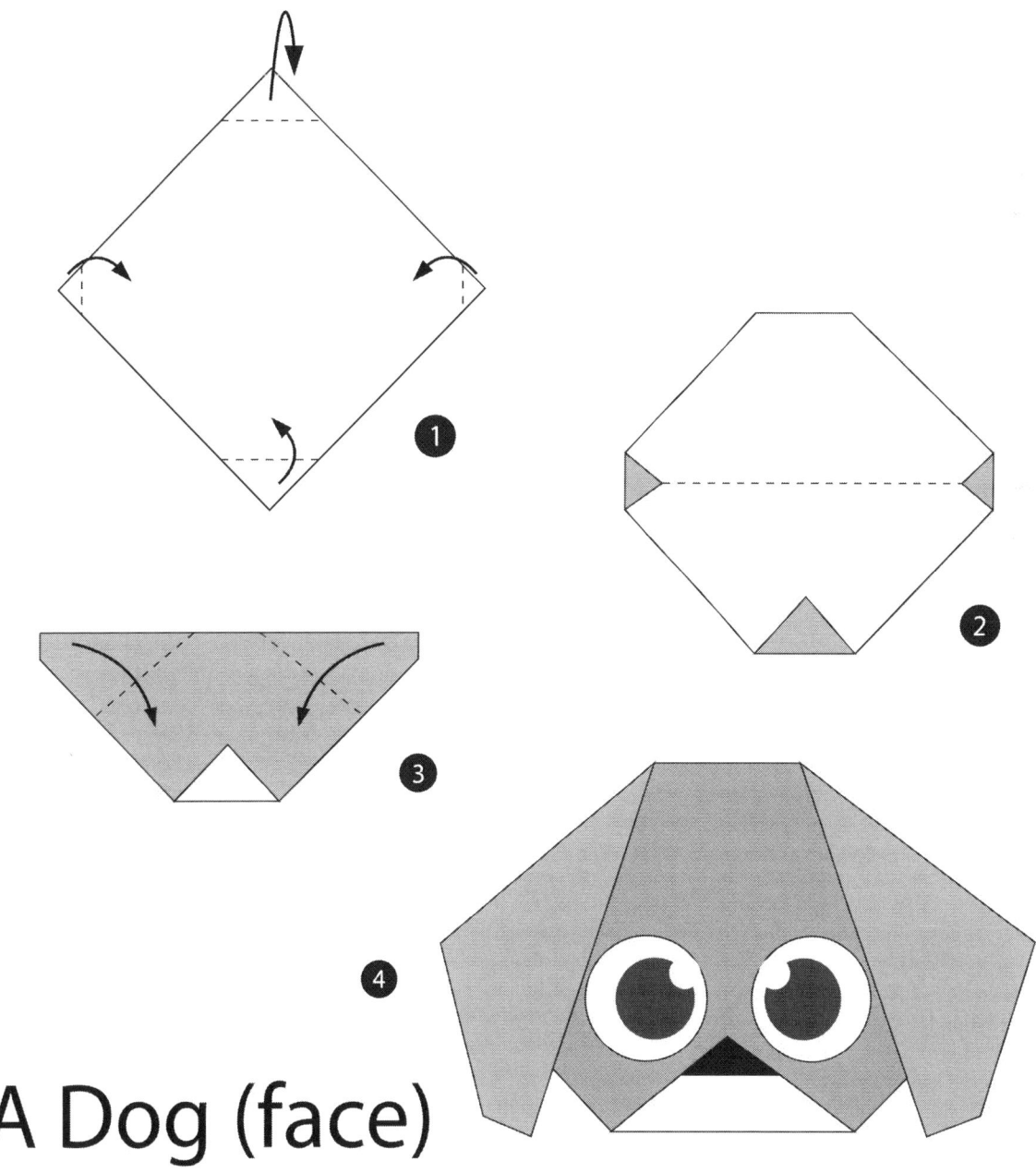

A Dog (face)

STORY WRITING TIME

If you can't think and write at the same time, record your story or ask someone older for help.

Title:

_____

Names & Descriptions of Characters:

_____
_____
_____
_____
_____

Base your story on the picture to the left.

_____
_____
_____
_____
_____
_____
_____
_____
_____
_____
_____
_____
_____
_____
_____
_____

DRAW MY HABITAT

CURSIVE WRITING PRACTICE

A B C D E F G
H I J K L M
N O P Q R S T
U V W X Y Z

a b c d e f g h
i j k l m n o p
q r s t u v w x
y z 1 2 3 4 5 6 7 8 9 0

ANIMAL TRACKS

CAT JAGUAR LION TIGER

DOG FOX WOLF BEAR

 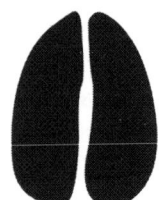 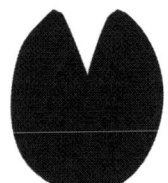 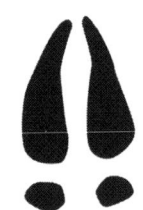

SHEEP COW HORSE DEER

KANGAROO LIZARD HIPPOPOTAMUS ELEPHANT

HOW MANY ANIMAL TRACKS CAN YOU DRAW?

SPELLING TIME

Choose a Letter: ___

Find 15 words that begin or end with that letter.

Five Nouns:

_____

_____

_____

_____

_____

Five Adjectives:

_____

_____

_____

_____

_____

Three Animals:

_____

_____

_____

Two Verbs:

_____

_____

Write a silly story, poem, song or play using words from your spelling list.

_____

_____

_____

_____

_____

_____

_____

_____

_____

_____

_____

_____

_____

_____

_____

_____

_____

_____

_____

CREATE A COMIC STRIP

Use your spelling words.

WHAT DID YOU LEARN ABOUT HISTORY TODAY?

WHAT DID YOU LEARN ABOUT SCIENCE TODAY?

WILDLIFE & GEOGRAPHY

RESEARCH AN ANIMAL OF YOUR CHOICE: _____

WHERE IN THE WORLD DOES THIS ANIMAL LIVE?

FUN FACTS:

DRAW THE ANIMAL:

FIELD TRIPS & BACKYARD SCIENCE

Go somewhere and draw what you see! Look for animals!

If you can't go very far, go to a park or your own backyard.

Today's Date: _____

Today I Saw: _____

_____

_____

CURSIVE WRITING PRACTICE

A B C D E F G
H I J K L M
N O P Q R S T
U V W X Y Z

a b c d e f g h
i j k l m n o p
q r s t u v w x
y z 1 2 3 4 5 6 7 8 9 0

SPELLING TIME

Choose an Animal

_____

Look in your books for 10 words that have some of the same letters as this animal.

1. _____
2. _____
3. _____
4. _____
5. _____
6. _____
7. _____
8. _____
9. _____
10. _____

ANIMAL QUIZ

I am _____

I live in _____

I like to eat _____

My enemies are _____

MOVIE TIME

Watch a movie or documentary about animals.

TITLE:_____

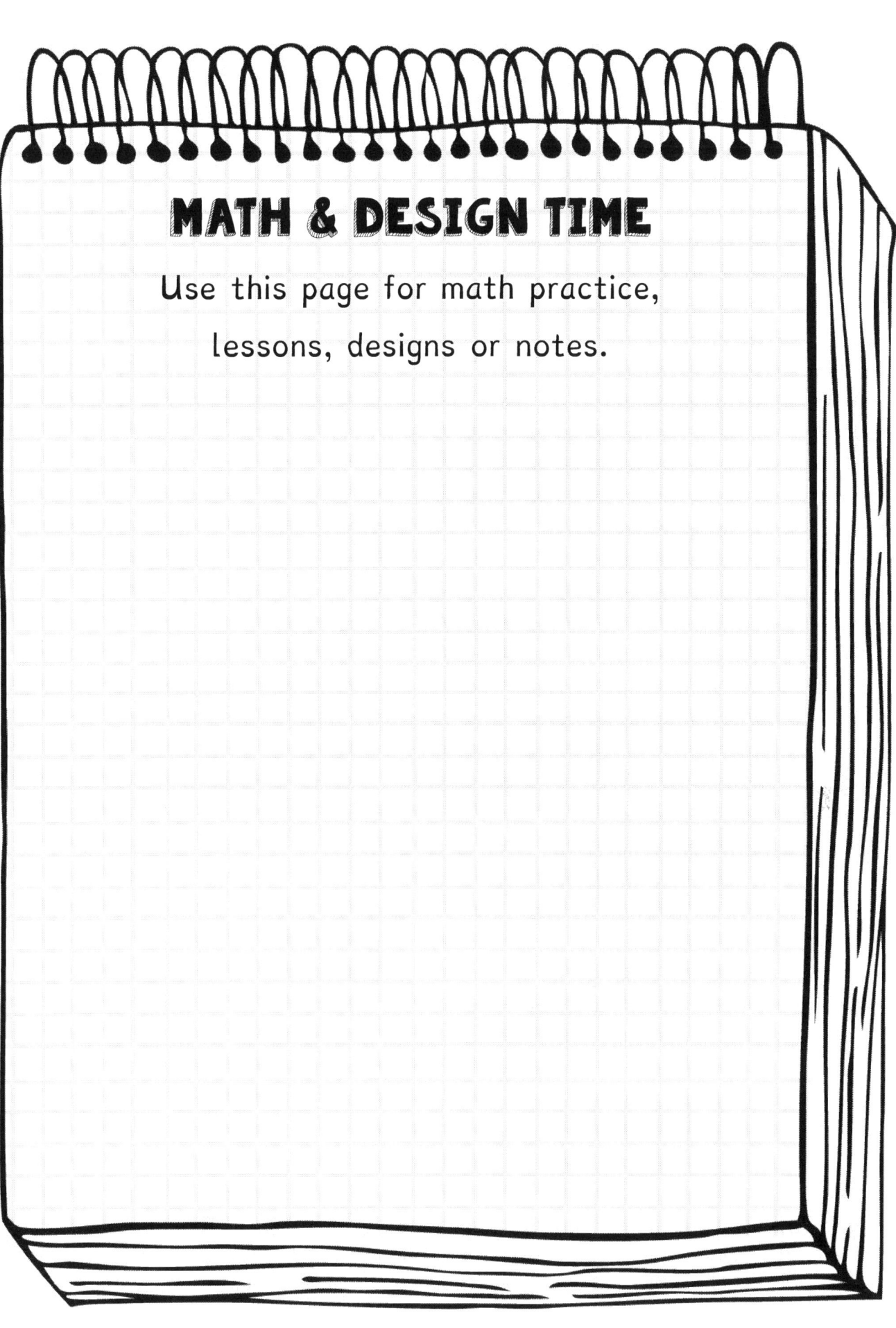

MATH & DESIGN TIME

Use this page for math practice, lessons, designs or notes.

STORY WRITING TIME

If you can't think and write at the same time, record your story or ask someone older for help.

Title:

_____

Names & Descriptions of Characters:

_____
_____
_____
_____
_____

Base your story on the picture to the left.

_____
_____
_____
_____
_____
_____
_____
_____
_____
_____
_____
_____
_____
_____
_____
_____
_____
_____
_____
_____

Today's

Date:

TO-DO LIST

1. ______________________

2. ______________________

3. ______________________

4. ______________________

ABCDEFG
HIJKLMN
OPQRSTU
VWXYZ

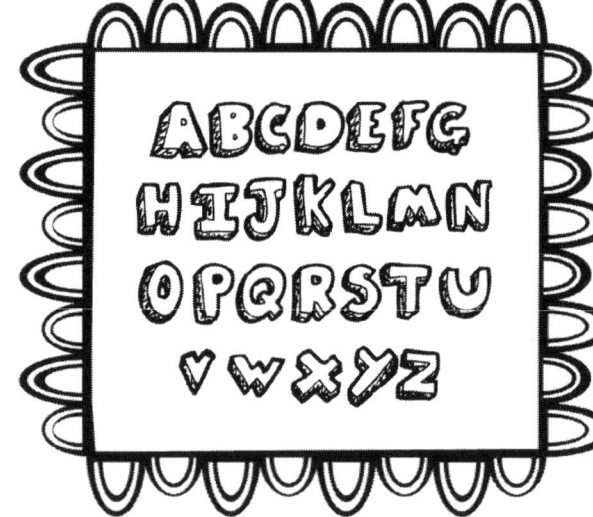

How are you

FEELING TODAY?

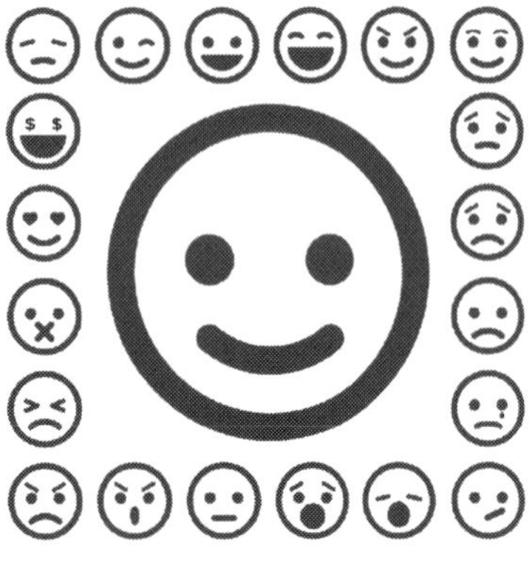

Draw a Pet

FIELD TRIPS & BACKYARD SCIENCE

Go somewhere and draw what you see! Look for animals!

If you can't go very far, go to a park or your own backyard.

Today's Date: _____

Today I Saw: _____
_____
_____
_____

Trace & Color

NUMBER SEARCH!

Find each number between 1 and 100

SPELLING TIME

Choose a Letter: ___

Find 15 words that begin or end with that letter.

Five Nouns:

_____
_____
_____
_____
_____

Five Adjectives:

_____
_____
_____
_____
_____

Three Animals:

_____
_____
_____

Two Verbs:

_____
_____

Write a silly story, poem, song or play using words from your spelling list.

_____
_____
_____
_____
_____
_____
_____
_____
_____
_____
_____
_____
_____
_____
_____
_____
_____

CREATE A COMIC STRIP

Use your spelling words.

Today's Date:
_____

READING TIME

Write and draw about what you are reading.

COPYWORK

Copy a paragraph from one of your library books.

TITLE: _____ Page#_____

_____

_____

_____

_____

_____

DRAWING TIME

Copy an illustration from one of your books.

BE CREATIVE
Draw Anything

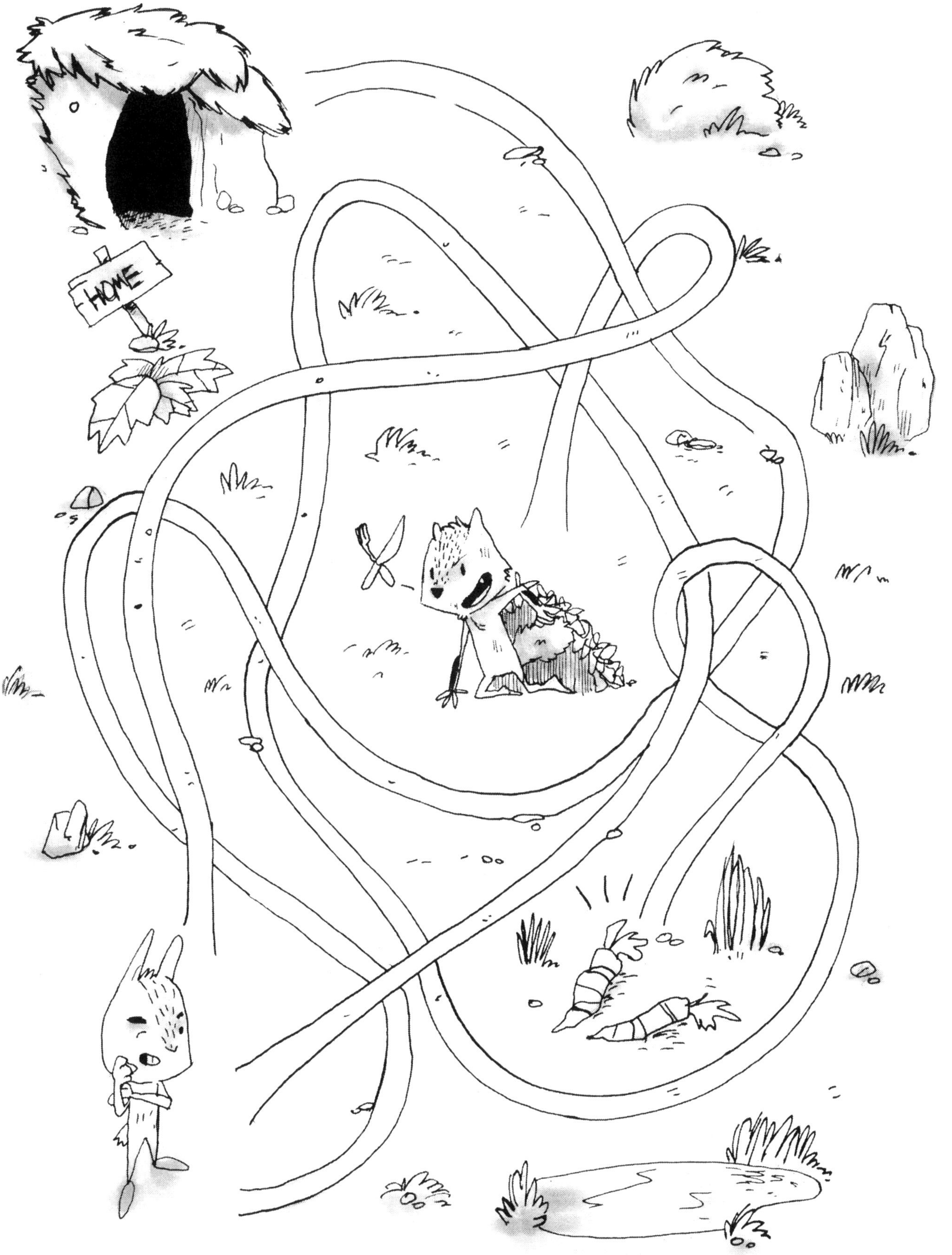
HOME

Today's Date:

TO-DO LIST

1._____

2._____

3._____

4._____

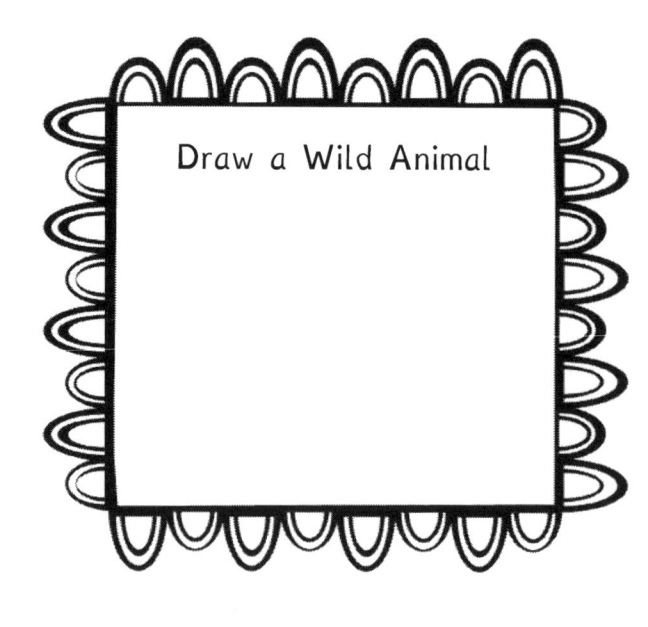

Draw a Wild Animal

How are you FEELING TODAY?

Draw a Pet

LISTENING TIME

CLASSICAL MUSIC & LITERATURE

Today's Date:_____

Listen to an audio book or classical music.

Draw and doodle below.

I am listening to: _____

WHAT DID YOU LEARN ABOUT HISTORY TODAY?

WHAT DID YOU LEARN ABOUT SCIENCE TODAY?

WILDLIFE & GEOGRAPHY

RESEARCH AN ANIMAL OF YOUR CHOICE: _____

WHERE IN THE WORLD DOES THIS ANIMAL LIVE?

FUN FACTS:

DRAW THE ANIMAL:

Today's Date:
_____

READING TIME

Write and draw about what you are reading.

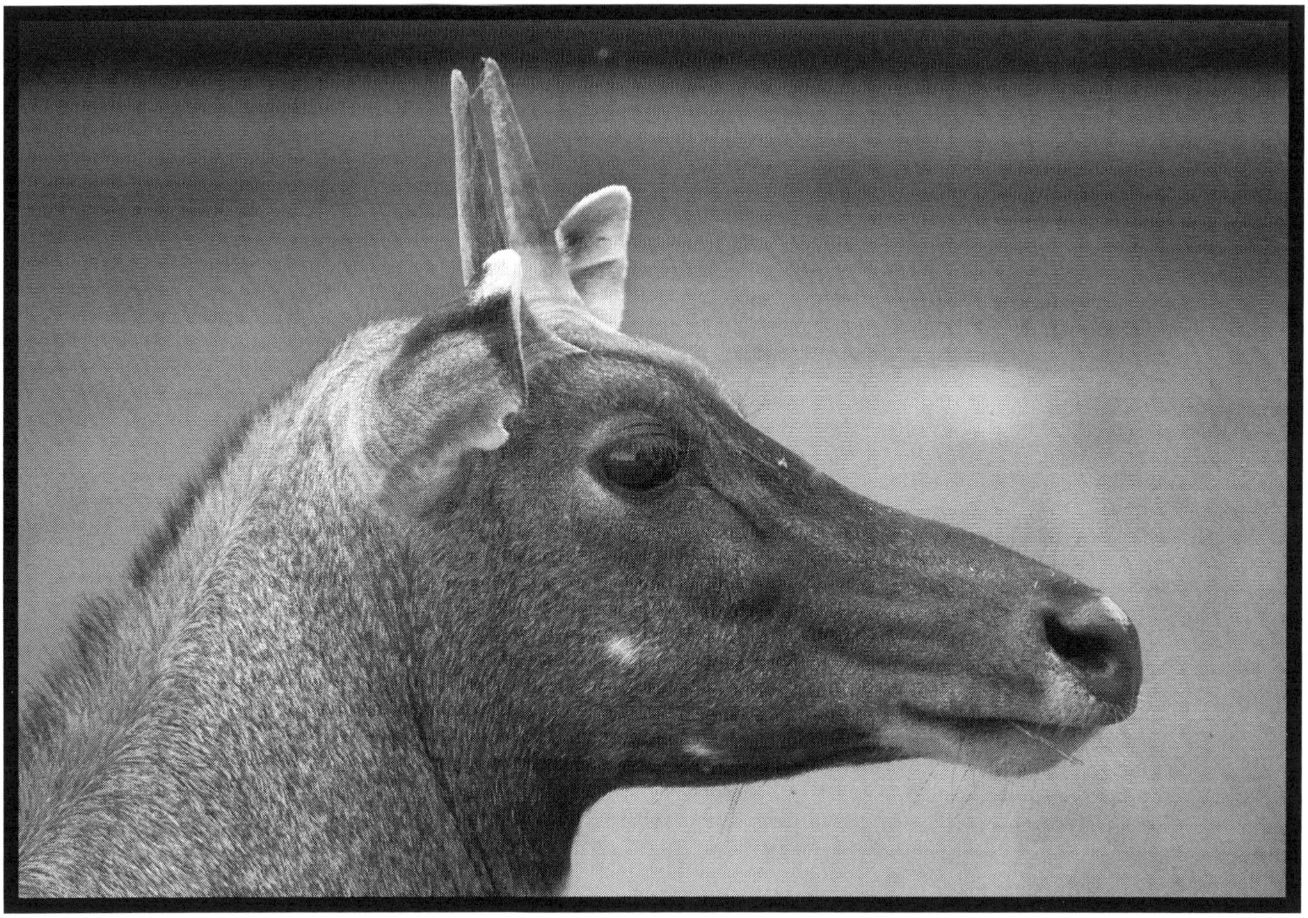

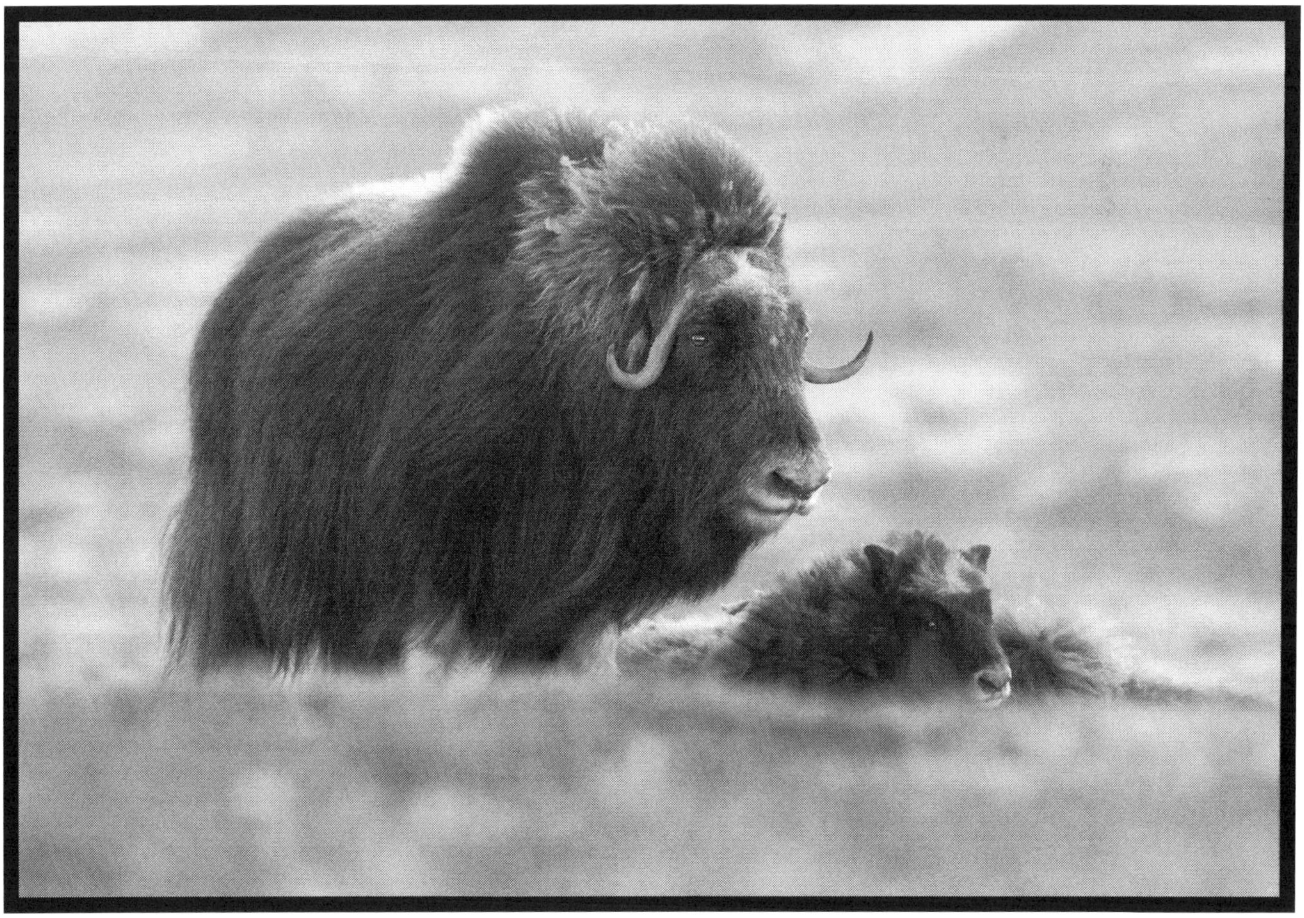

CURSIVE WRITING PRACTICE

A B C D E F G
H I J K L M
N O P Q R S T
U V W X Y Z

a b c d e f g h
i j k l m n o p
q r s t u v w x
y z 1 2 3 4 5 6 7 8 9 0

FIELD TRIPS & BACKYARD SCIENCE

Go somewhere and draw what you see! Look for animals!

If you can't go very far, go to a park or your own backyard.

Today's Date: _____

Today I Saw: _____

_____

_____

MOVIE TIME

Watch a movie or documentary about animals.

TITLE:_____

Draw Your Favorite Scenes:

RATING

ORIGAMI CHALLENGE
CAN YOU MAKE THIS ANIMAL?

Set a timer.

Minutes:_____   Seconds:_____

A Gorilla

Today's Date:

TO-DO LIST

1._____

2._____

3._____

4._____

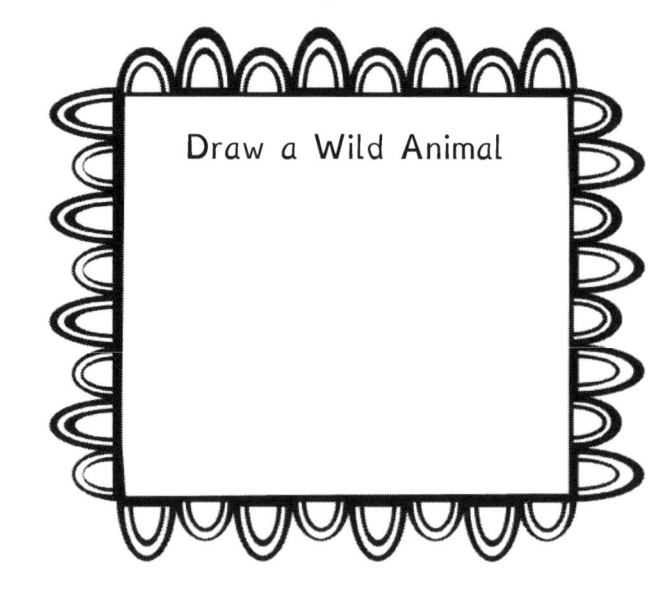

Draw a Wild Animal

How are you FEELING TODAY?

Draw a Pet

ANIMAL QUIZ

I am _____

I live in _____

I like to eat _____

My enemies are _____

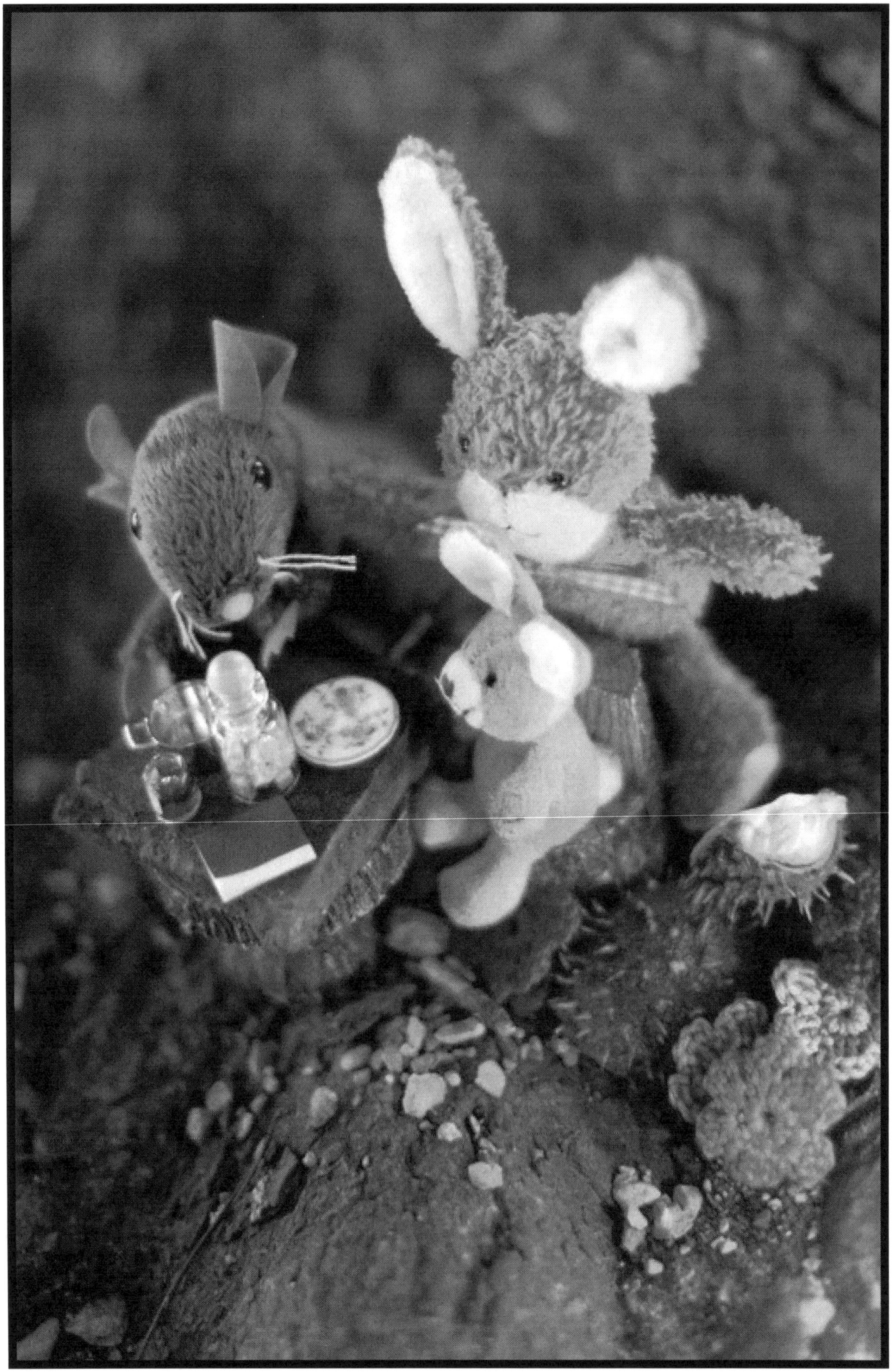

STORY WRITING TIME

If you can't think and write at the same time, record your story or ask someone older for help.

Title:

_____

Names & Descriptions of Characters:

_____
_____
_____
_____
_____

Base your story on the picture to the left.

_____
_____
_____
_____
_____
_____
_____
_____
_____
_____
_____
_____
_____
_____
_____
_____

SPELLING TIME

Choose a Letter: ___

Find 15 words that begin or end with that letter.

Five Nouns:

_____
_____
_____
_____
_____

Five Adjectives:

_____
_____
_____
_____
_____

Three Animals:

_____
_____
_____

Two Verbs:

_____
_____

Write a silly story, poem, song or play using words from your spelling list.

_____
_____
_____
_____
_____
_____
_____
_____
_____
_____
_____
_____
_____
_____
_____
_____
_____
_____
_____
_____

CREATE A COMIC STRIP

Use your spelling words.

Today's Date:

READING TIME

Write and draw about what you are reading.

CURSIVE WRITING PRACTICE

A B C D E F G
H I J K L M
N O P Q R S T
U V W X Y Z

a b c d e f g h
i j k l m n o p
q r s t u v w x
y z 1 2 3 4 5 6 7 8 9 0

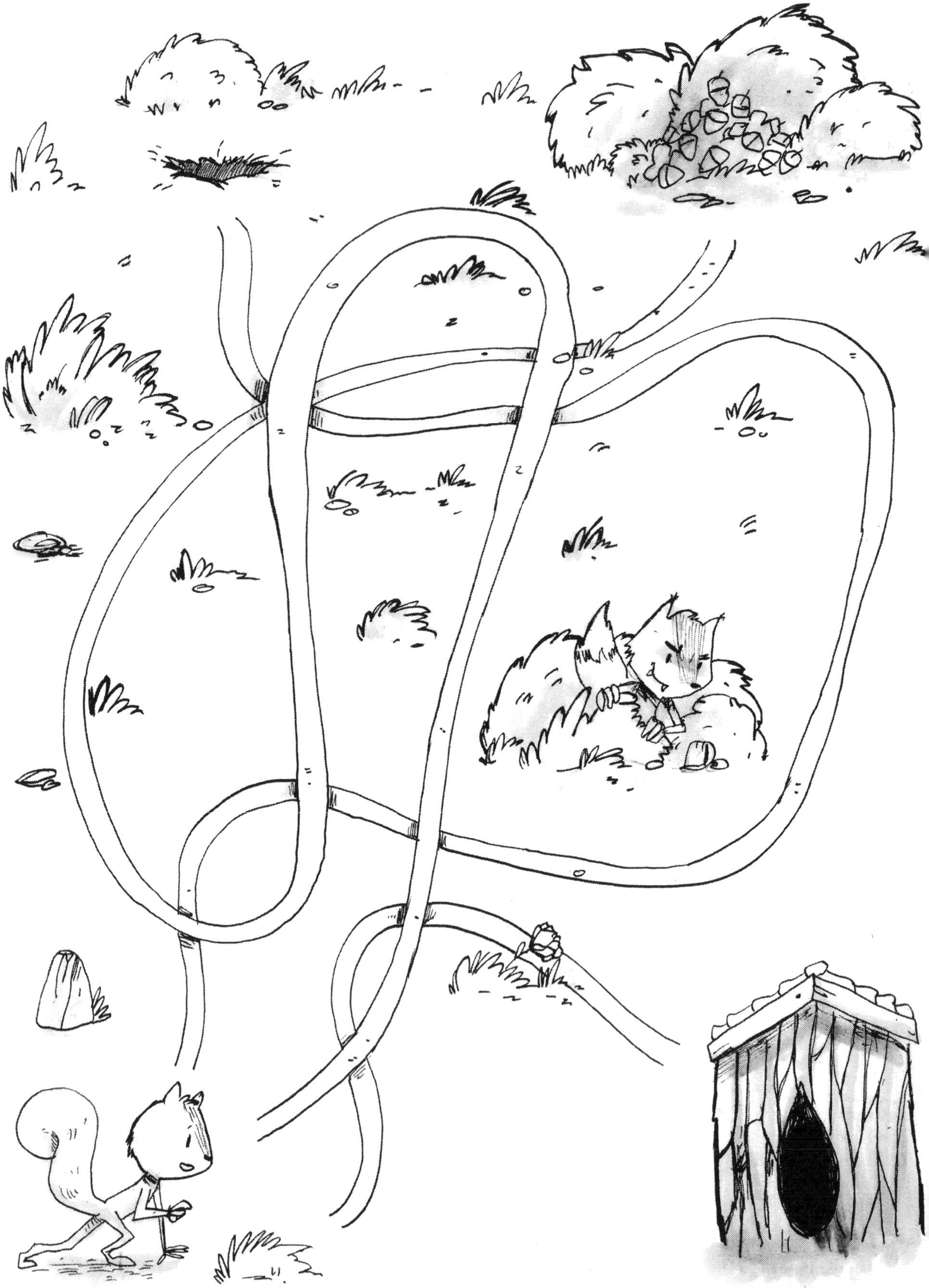

SPELLING TIME

Choose an Animal

_____

Look in your books for 10 words that have some of the same letters as this animal.

1._____

2._____

3._____

4._____

5._____

6._____

7._____

8._____

9._____

10._____

WHAT DID YOU LEARN ABOUT HISTORY TODAY?

WHAT DID YOU LEARN ABOUT SCIENCE TODAY?

WILDLIFE & GEOGRAPHY

RESEARCH AN ANIMAL OF YOUR CHOICE: _____

WHERE IN THE WORLD DOES THIS ANIMAL LIVE?

FUN FACTS:

DRAW THE ANIMAL:

Today's Date:

TO-DO LIST

1._____

2._____

3._____

4._____

How are you FEELING TODAY?

ABCDEFG
HIJKLMN
OPQRSTU
VWXYZ

Draw a Pet

CREATIVE WRITING

Write a short story about this picture. Ask someone older to help you write the words.

Today's Date:
_____

READING TIME

Write and draw about what you are reading.

FIELD TRIPS & BACKYARD SCIENCE

Go somewhere and draw what you see! Look for animals!

If you can't go very far, go to a park or your own backyard.

Today's Date: _____

Today I Saw: _____

_____

_____

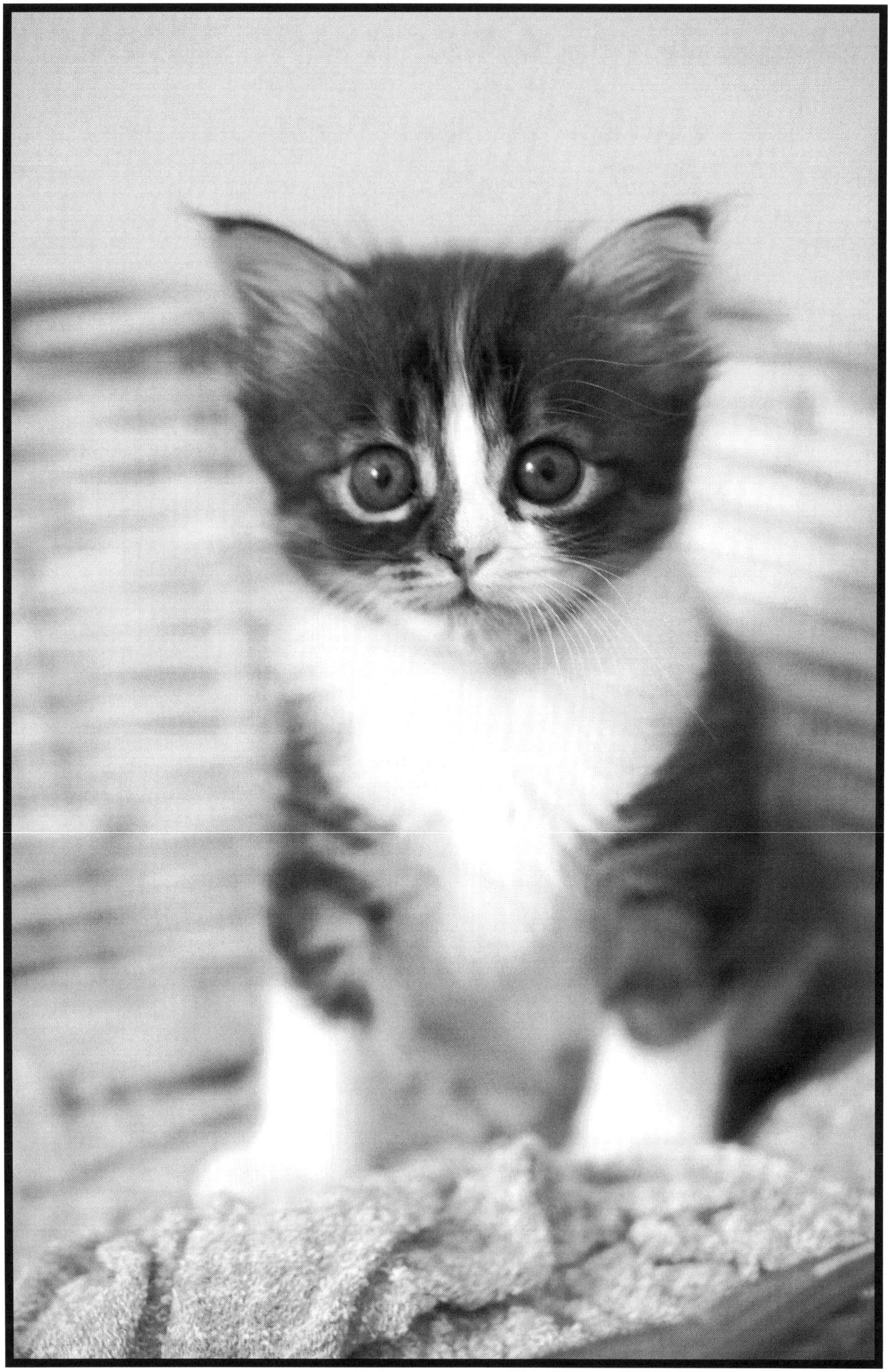

Trace & Color

MOVIE TIME

Watch a movie or documentary about animals.

TITLE:_____

Draw Your Favorite Scenes:

RATING

ORIGAMI CHALLENGE
CAN YOU MAKE THIS ANIMAL?

Set a timer.

Minutes:_____   Seconds:_____

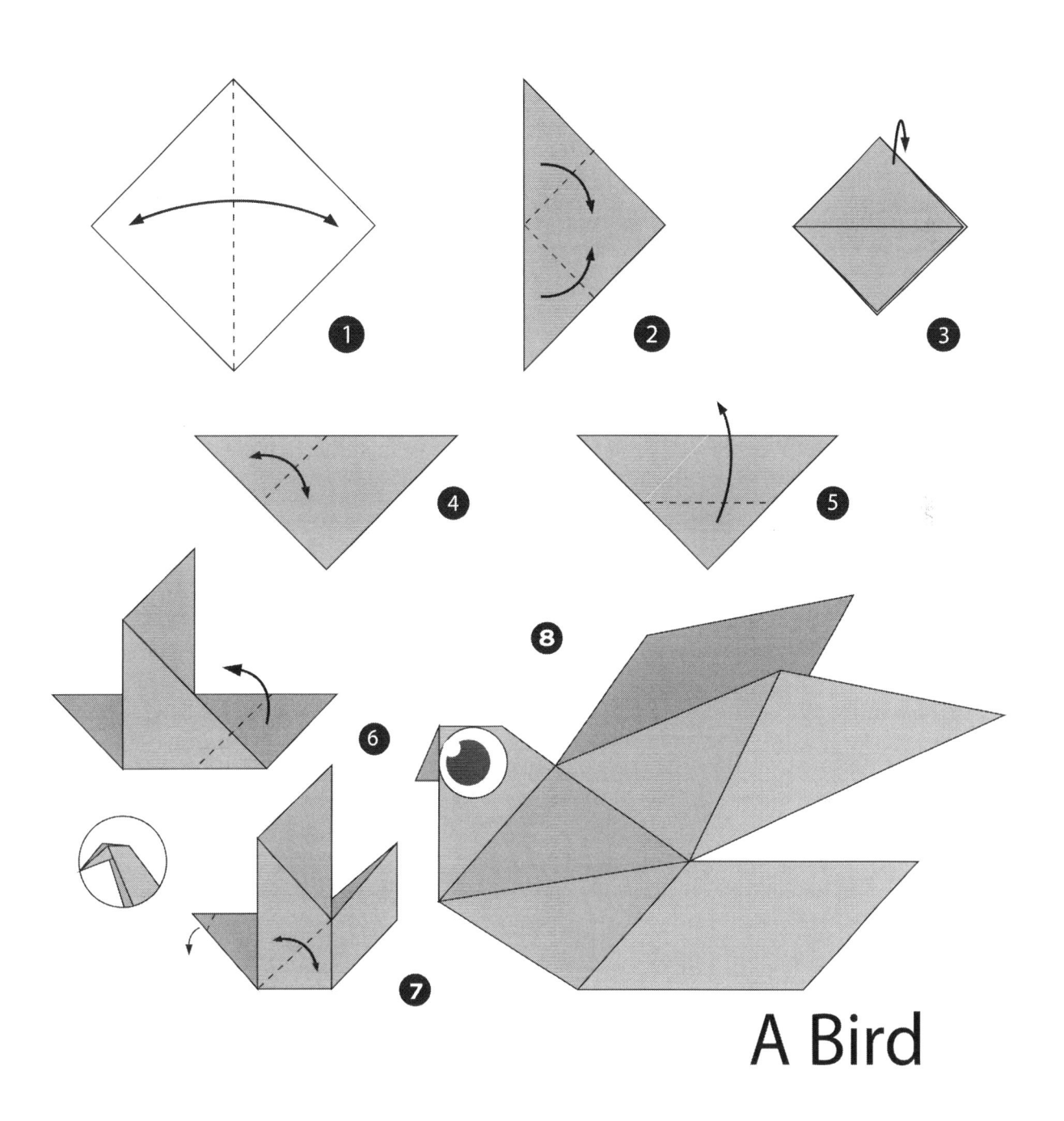

A Bird

SPELLING TIME

Choose an Animal

_____

Look in your books for 10 words that have some of the same letters as this animal.

1. _____
2. _____
3. _____
4. _____
5. _____
6. _____
7. _____
8. _____
9. _____
10. _____

ANIMAL QUIZ

I am _____

I live in _____

I like to eat _____

My enemies are _____

Today's Date:

TO-DO LIST

1._____

2._____

3._____

4._____

Draw a Wild Animal

How are you FEELING TODAY?

Draw a Pet

FIELD TRIPS & BACKYARD SCIENCE

Go somewhere and draw what you see! Look for animals!

If you can't go very far, go to a park or your own backyard.

Today's Date: _____

Today I Saw: _____

_____

_____

SPELLING TIME

Choose a Letter: ___

Find 15 words that begin or end with that letter.

Five Nouns:

Write a silly story, poem, song or play using words from your spelling list.

Five Adjectives:

Three Animals:

Two Verbs:

CREATE A COMIC STRIP

Use your spelling words.

Today's Date:
_____

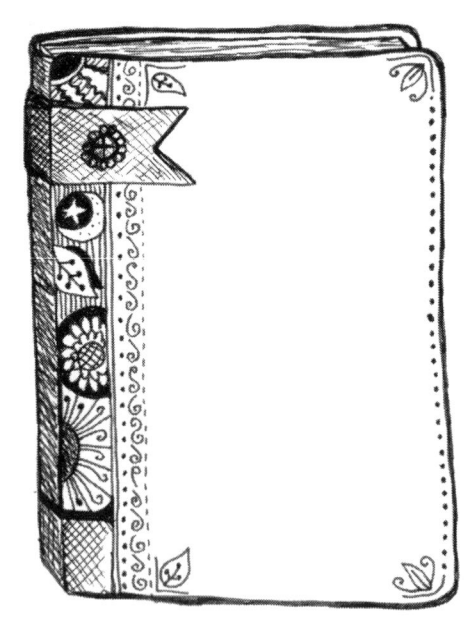

READING TIME

Write and draw about what you are reading.

COPYWORK

Copy a paragraph from one of your library books.

TITLE: _____ Page#_____

_____

_____

_____

_____

_____

DRAWING TIME

Copy an illustration from one of your books.

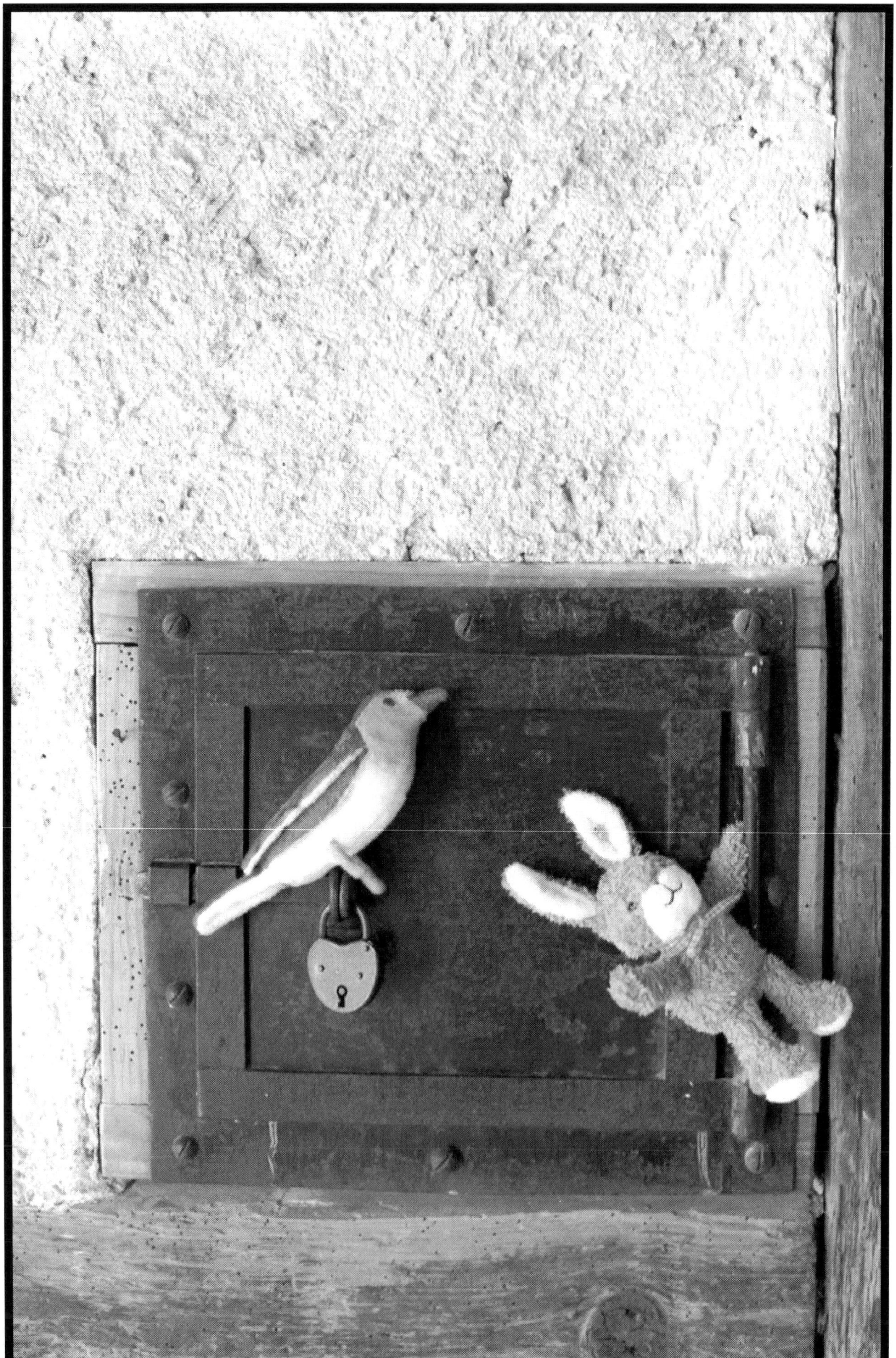

STORY WRITING TIME

If you can't think and write at the same time, record your story or ask someone older for help.

Title:

___

Names & Descriptions of Characters:

___

Base your story on the picture to the left.

___

CREATIVE WRITING

Write a short story about this picture. Ask someone older to help you write the words.

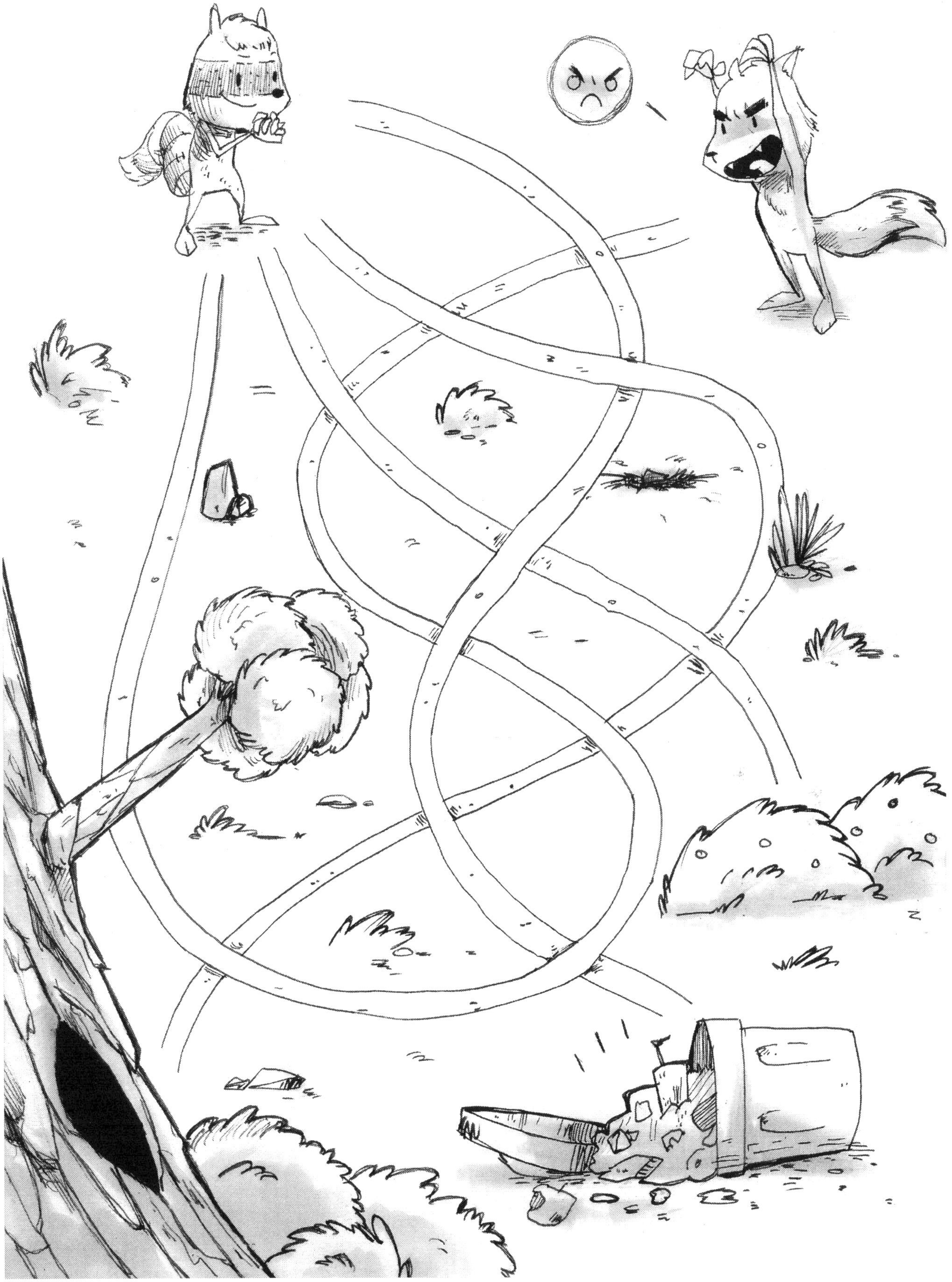

WHAT DID YOU LEARN ABOUT HISTORY TODAY?

WHAT DID YOU LEARN ABOUT SCIENCE TODAY?

WILDLIFE & GEOGRAPHY

RESEARCH AN ANIMAL OF YOUR CHOICE: _____

WHERE IN THE WORLD DOES THIS ANIMAL LIVE?

FUN FACTS:

DRAW THE ANIMAL:

MATH & DESIGN TIME

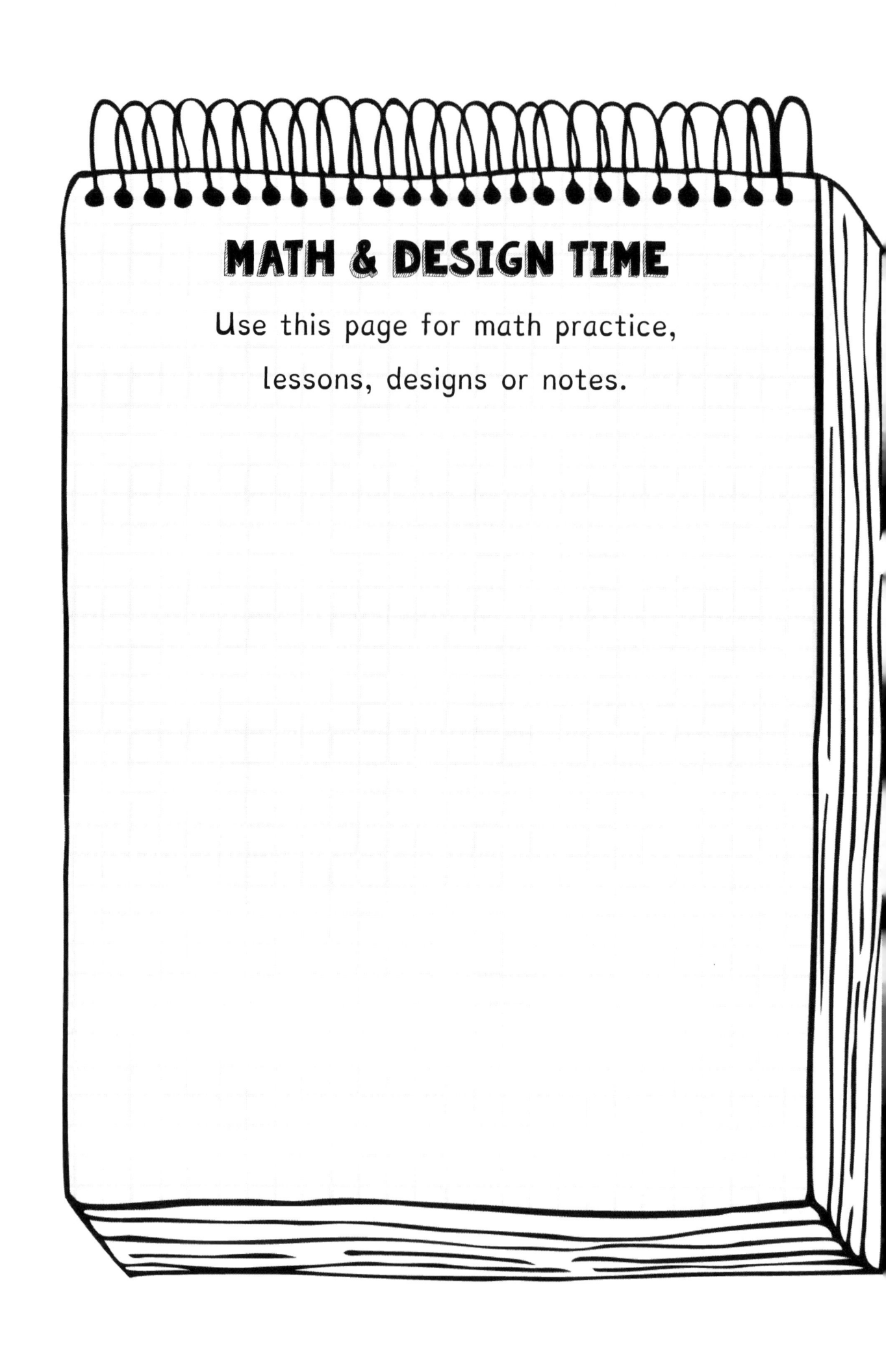

Use this page for math practice, lessons, designs or notes.

FINISH THE PICTURE:

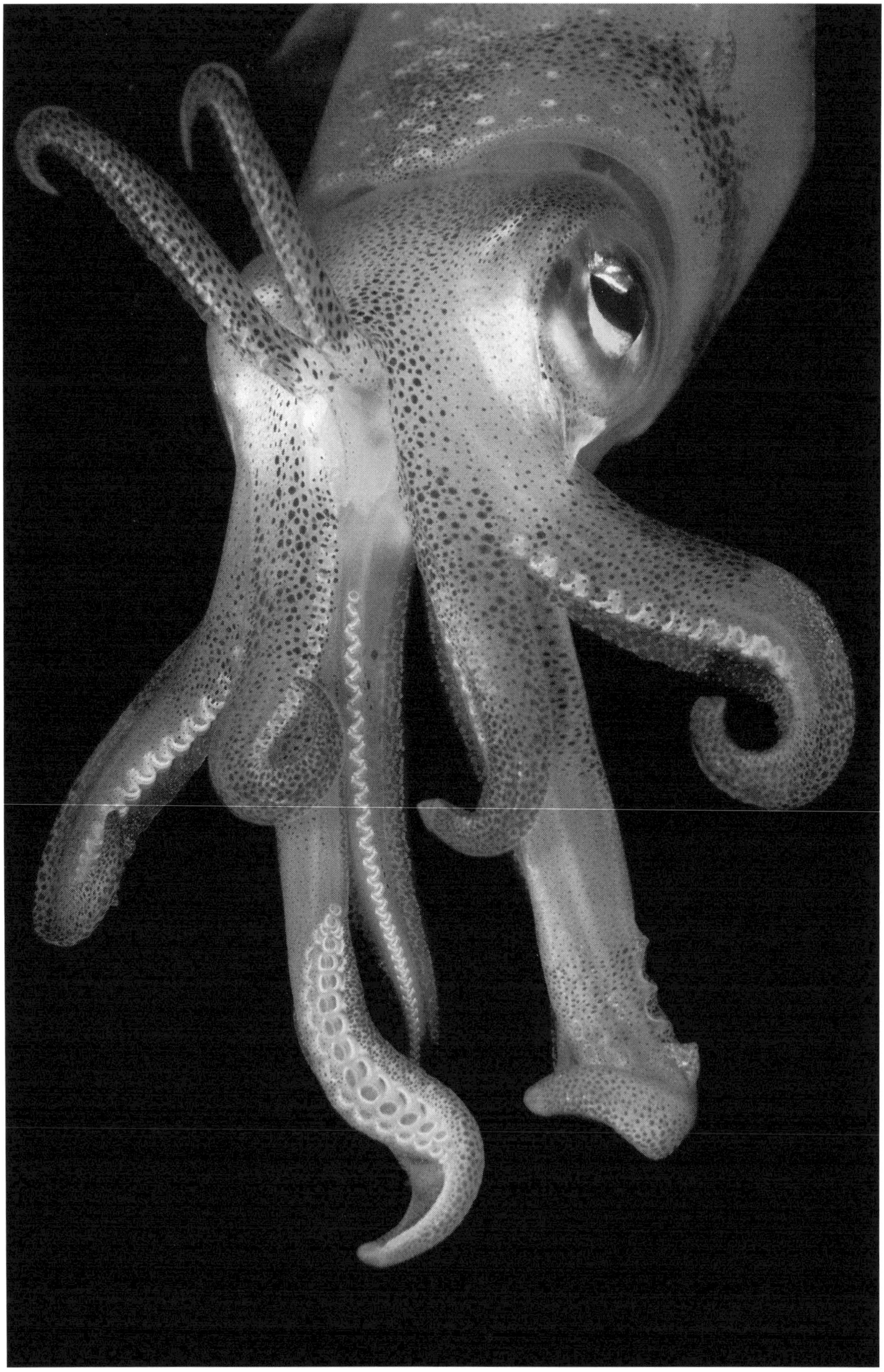

Today's Date:

TO-DO LIST

1._____

2._____

3._____

4._____

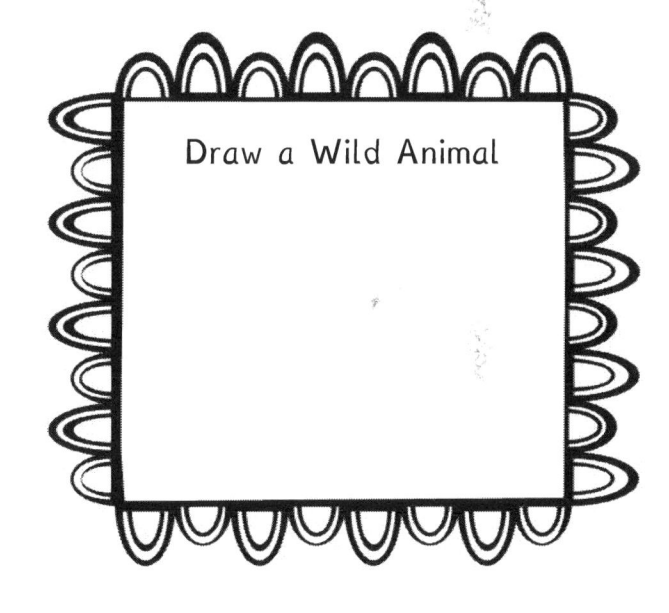

Draw a Wild Animal

How are you FEELING TODAY?

Draw a Pet

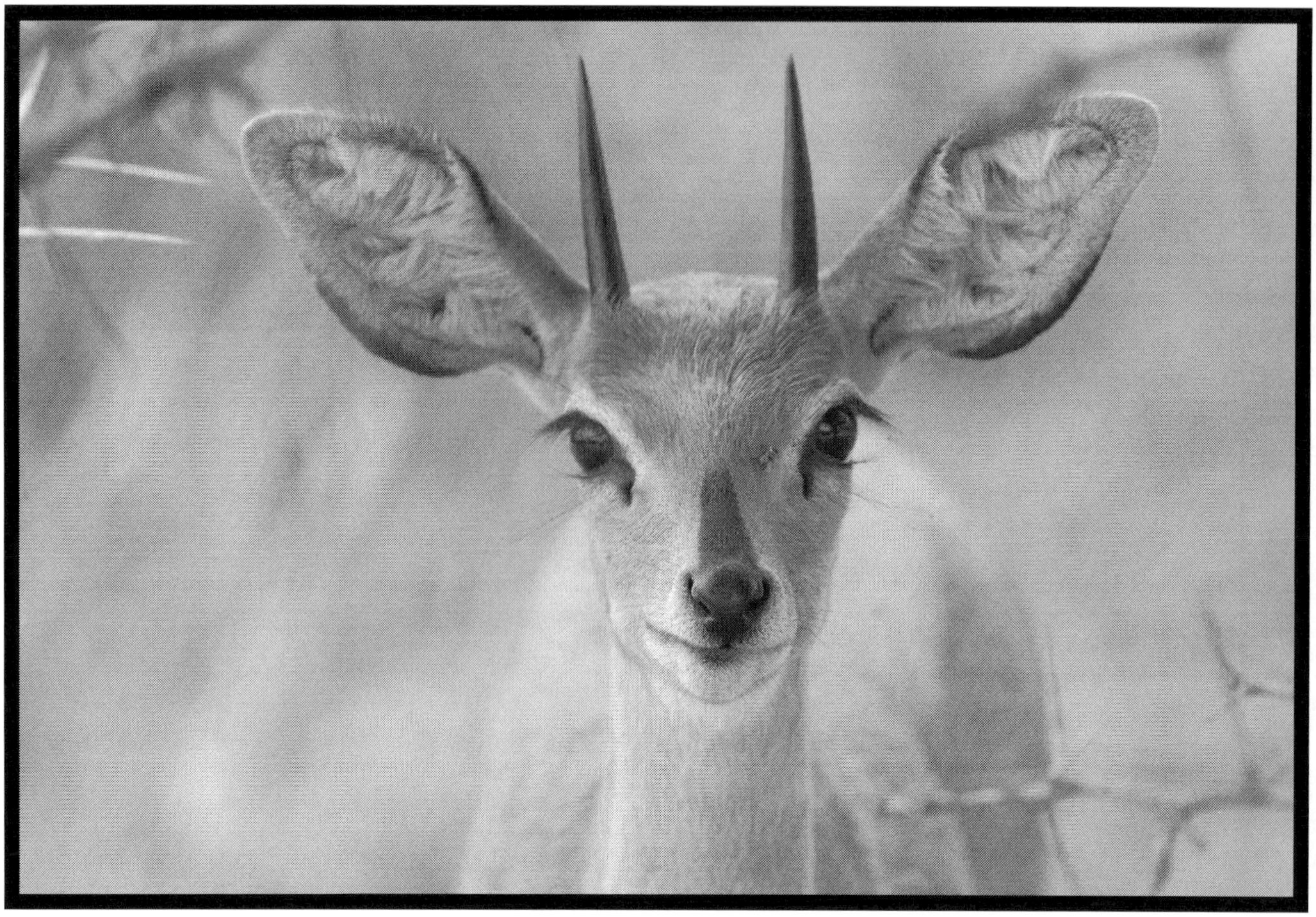

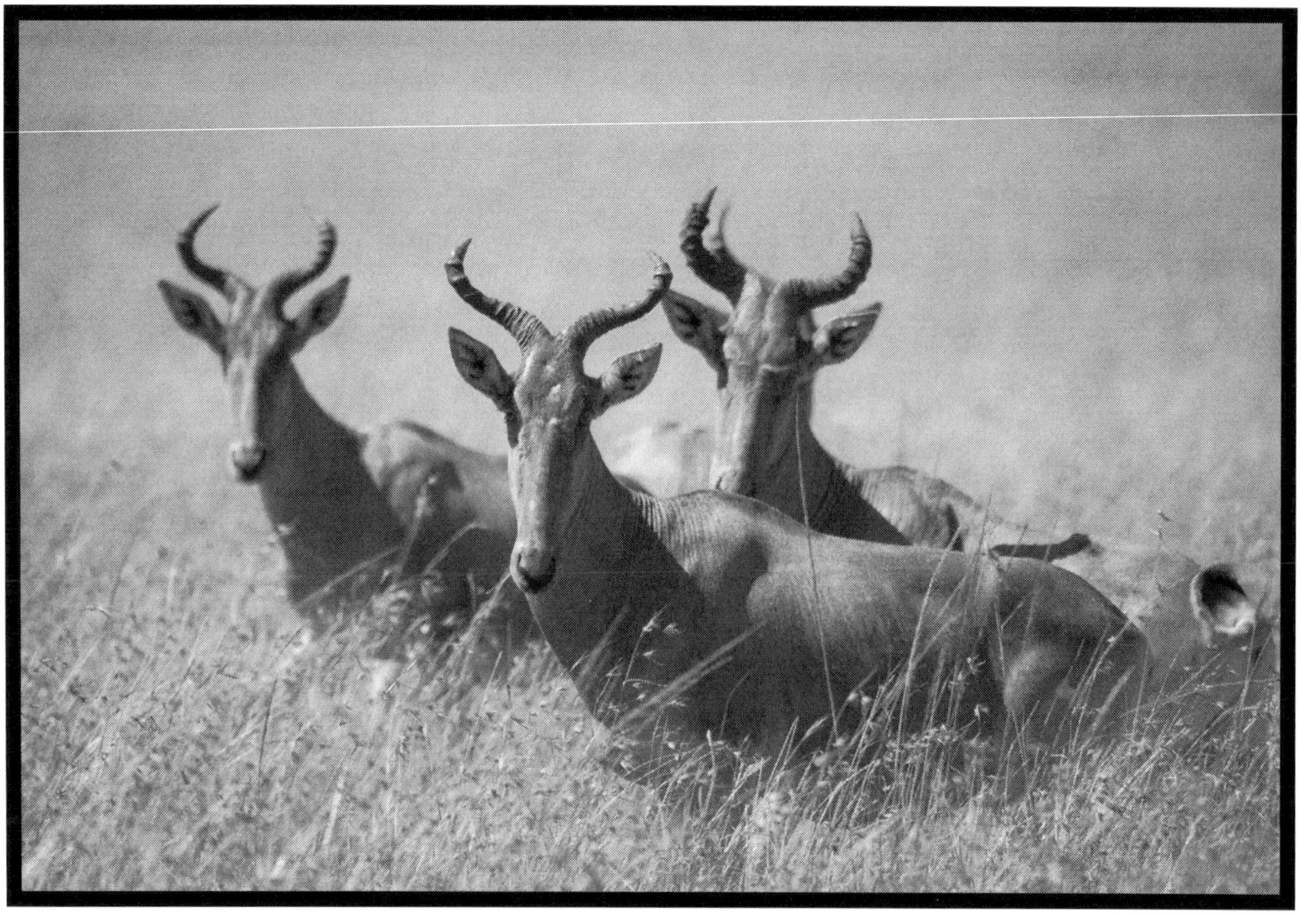

LISTENING TIME

CLASSICAL MUSIC & LITERATURE

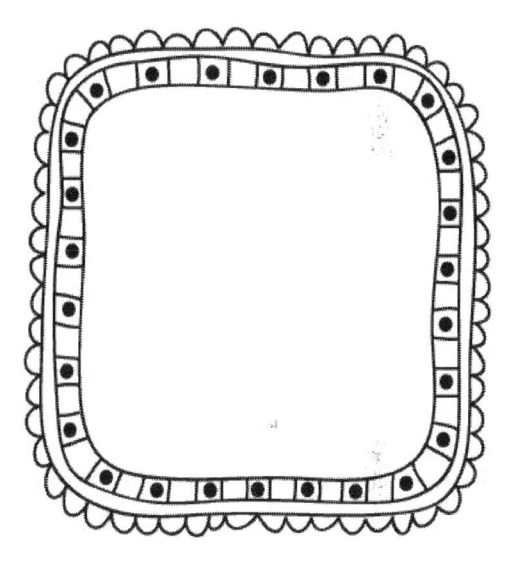

Today's Date:_____

Listen to an audio book or classical music.

Draw and doodle below.

I am listening to: _____

Today's Date:
_____

READING TIME

Write and draw about what you are reading.

FIELD TRIPS & BACKYARD SCIENCE

Go somewhere and draw what you see! Look for animals!

If you can't go very far, go to a park or your own backyard.

Today's Date: _____

Today I Saw: _____
_____
_____

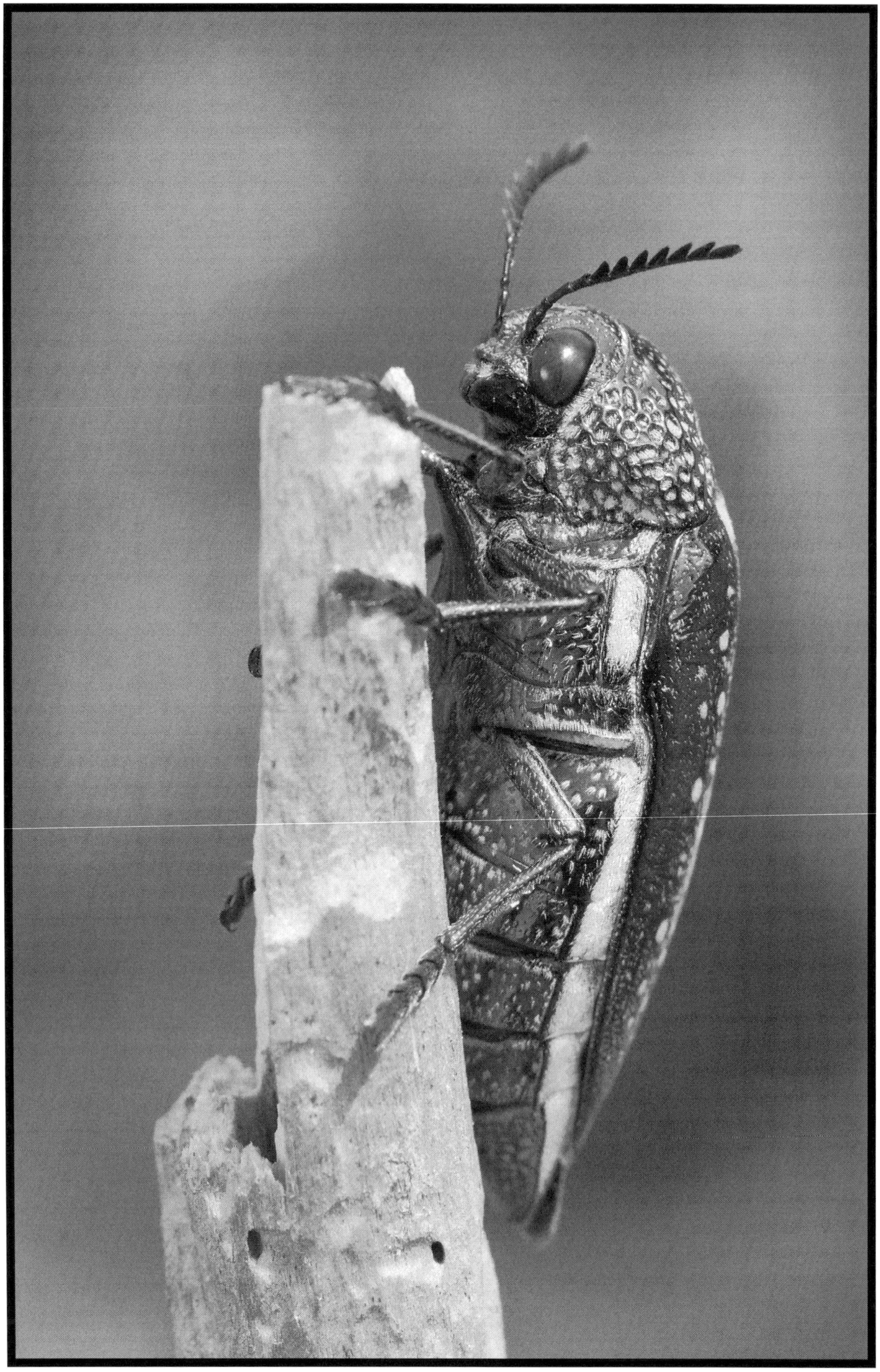

Trace & Color

SPELLING TIME

Choose a Letter: ___

Find 15 words that begin or end with that letter.

Five Nouns:

_____
_____
_____
_____
_____

Five Adjectives:

_____
_____
_____
_____
_____

Three Animals:

_____
_____
_____

Two Verbs:

_____
_____

Write a silly story, poem, song or play using words from your spelling list.

_____
_____
_____
_____
_____
_____
_____
_____
_____
_____
_____
_____
_____
_____
_____
_____
_____
_____
_____

CREATE A COMIC STRIP

Use your spelling words.

Draw & Doodle

CREATIVE WRITING

Write a short story about this picture. Ask someone older to help you write the words.

_____
_____
_____
_____
_____
_____
_____
_____
_____

MOVIE TIME

Watch a movie or documentary about animals.

TITLE:_____

Draw Your Favorite Scenes:

RATING

ANIMAL QUIZ

I am _____

I live in _____

I like to eat _____

My enemies are _____

Today's Date:

TO-DO LIST

1._____

2._____

3._____

4._____

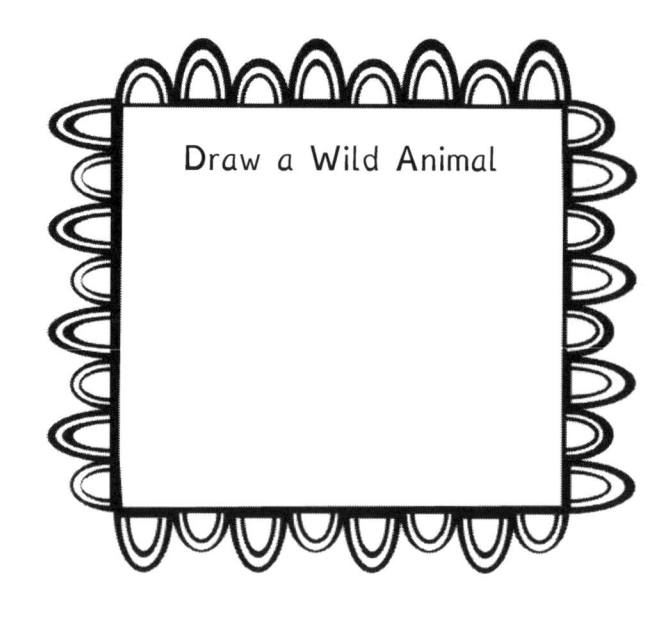

Draw a Wild Animal

How are you FEELING TODAY?

Draw a Pet

DRAW MY HABITAT

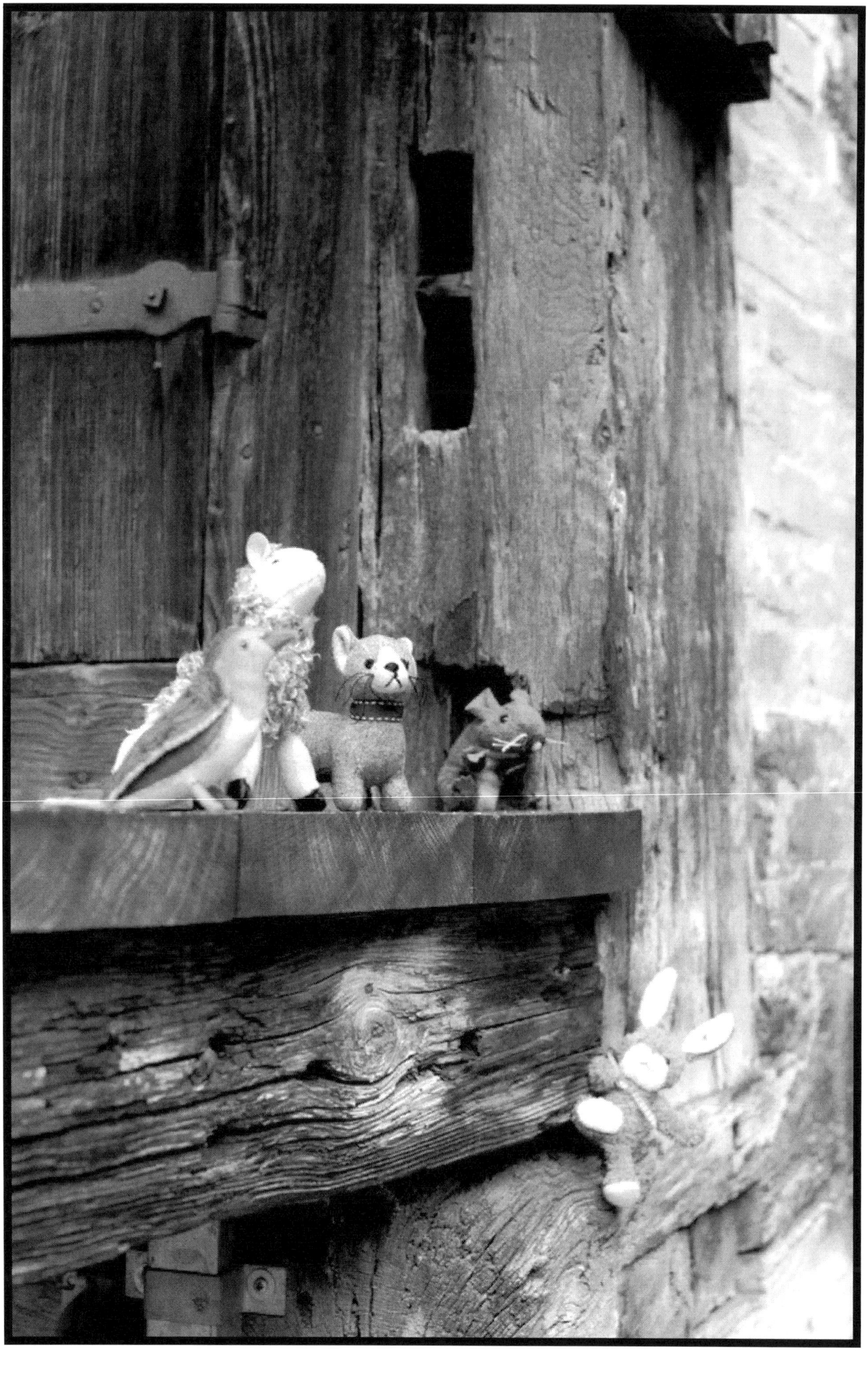

STORY WRITING TIME

If you can't think and write at the same time, record your story or ask someone older for help.

Title:

Names & Descriptions of Characters:

Base your story on the picture to the left.

WHAT DID YOU LEARN ABOUT HISTORY TODAY?

WHAT DID YOU LEARN ABOUT SCIENCE TODAY?

WILDLIFE & GEOGRAPHY

RESEARCH AN ANIMAL OF YOUR CHOICE: _____

WHERE IN THE WORLD DOES THIS ANIMAL LIVE?

FUN FACTS:

DRAW THE ANIMAL:

Today's Date:
_____

READING TIME

Write and draw about what you are reading.

FIELD TRIPS & BACKYARD SCIENCE

Go somewhere and draw what you see! Look for animals!

If you can't go very far, go to a park or your own backyard.

Today's Date: _____

Today I Saw: _____

_____

_____

_____

CURSIVE WRITING PRACTICE

A B C D E F G
H I J K L M
N O P Q R S T
U V W X Y Z

a b c d e f g h
i j k l m n o p
q r s t u v w x
y z 1 2 3 4 5 6 7 8 9 0

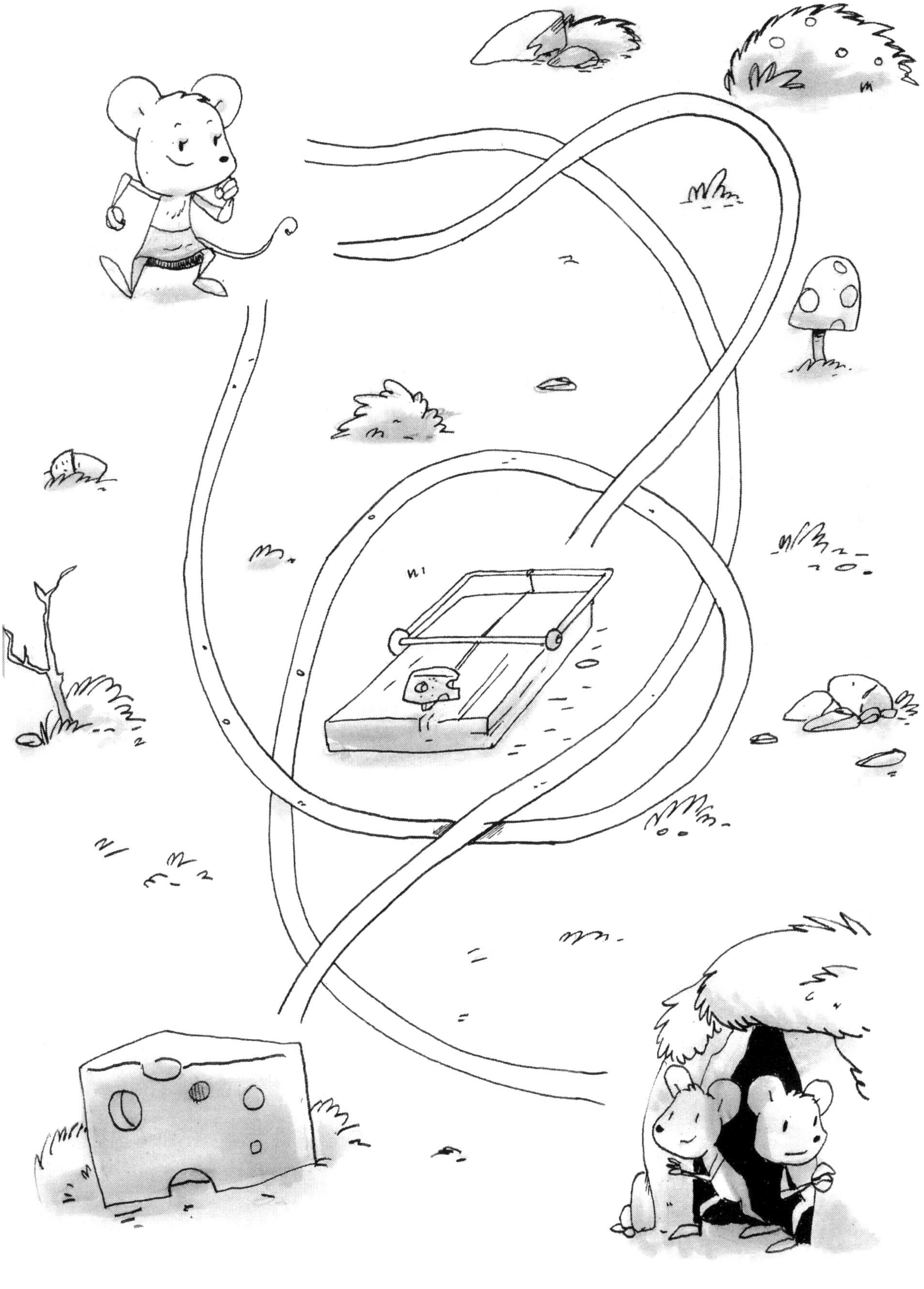

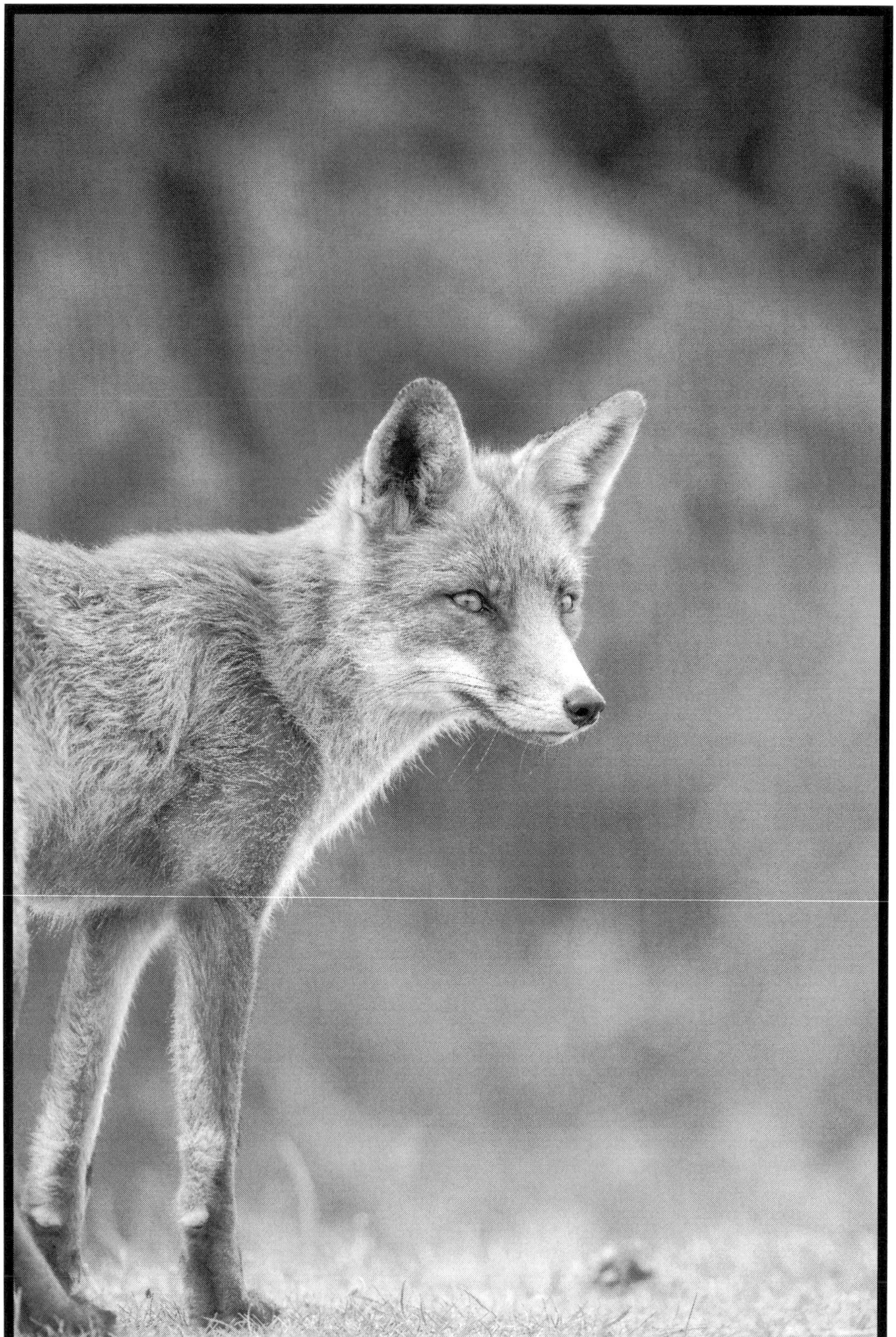

Trace & Color

DRAW MY HABITAT

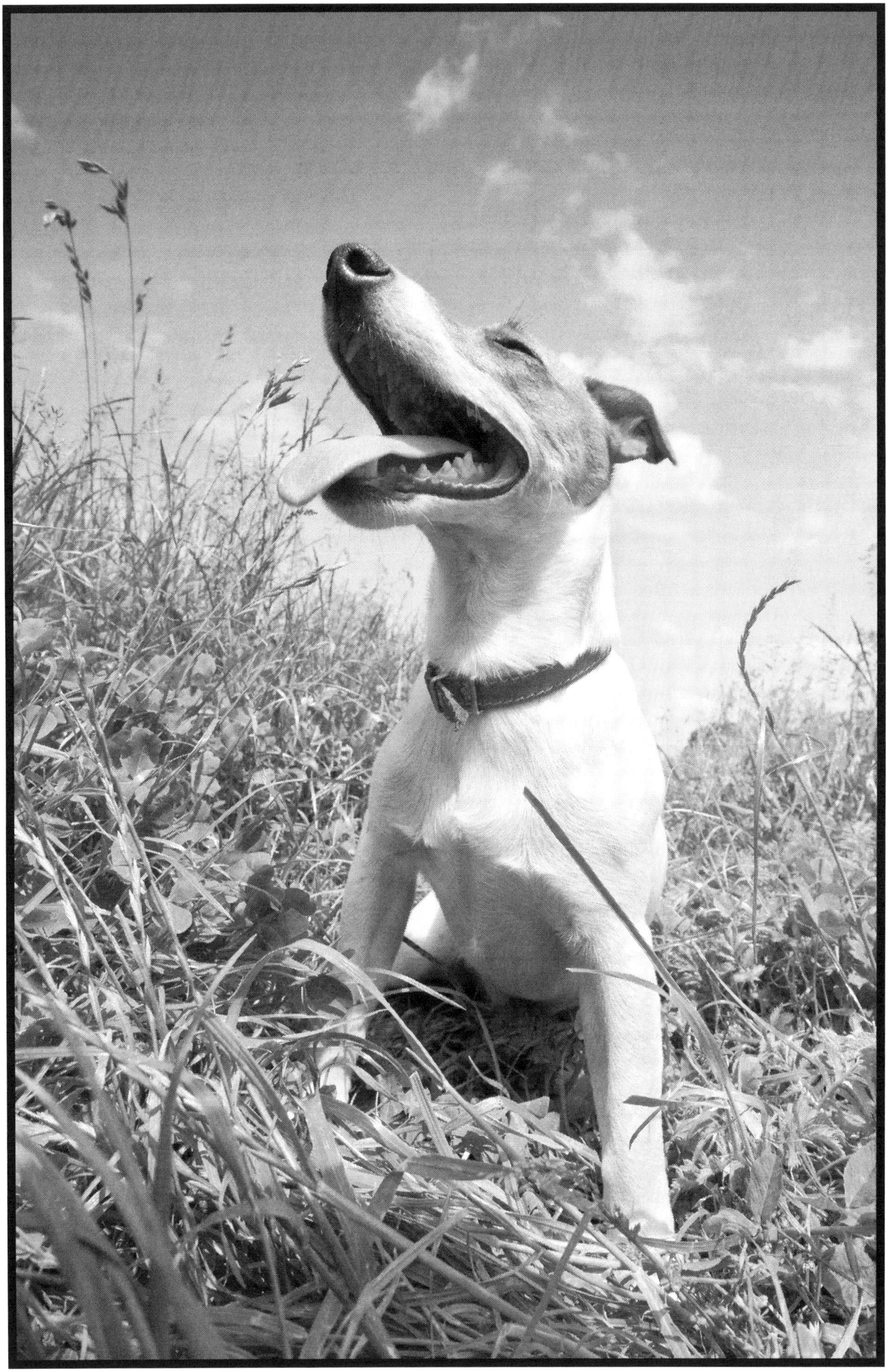

SPELLING TIME

Choose a Letter: ___

Find 15 words that begin or end with that letter.

Five Nouns:

_____

_____

_____

_____

_____

Five Adjectives:

_____

_____

_____

_____

_____

Three Animals:

_____

_____

_____

Two Verbs:

_____

_____

Write a silly story, poem, song or play using words from your spelling list.

CREATE A COMIC STRIP

Use your spelling words.

Today's Date:

TO-DO LIST

1._____
2._____
3._____
4._____

ABCDEFG
HIJKLMN
OPQRSTU
VWXYZ

How are you FEELING TODAY?

Draw a Pet

DRAW MY HABITAT

Today's Date:

READING TIME

Write and draw about what you are reading.

CREATIVE WRITING

Write a short story about this picture. Ask someone older to help you write the words.

SPELLING TIME

Choose an Animal

_____

Look in your books for 10 words that have some of the same letters as this animal.

1. _____
2. _____
3. _____
4. _____
5. _____
6. _____
7. _____
8. _____
9. _____
10. _____

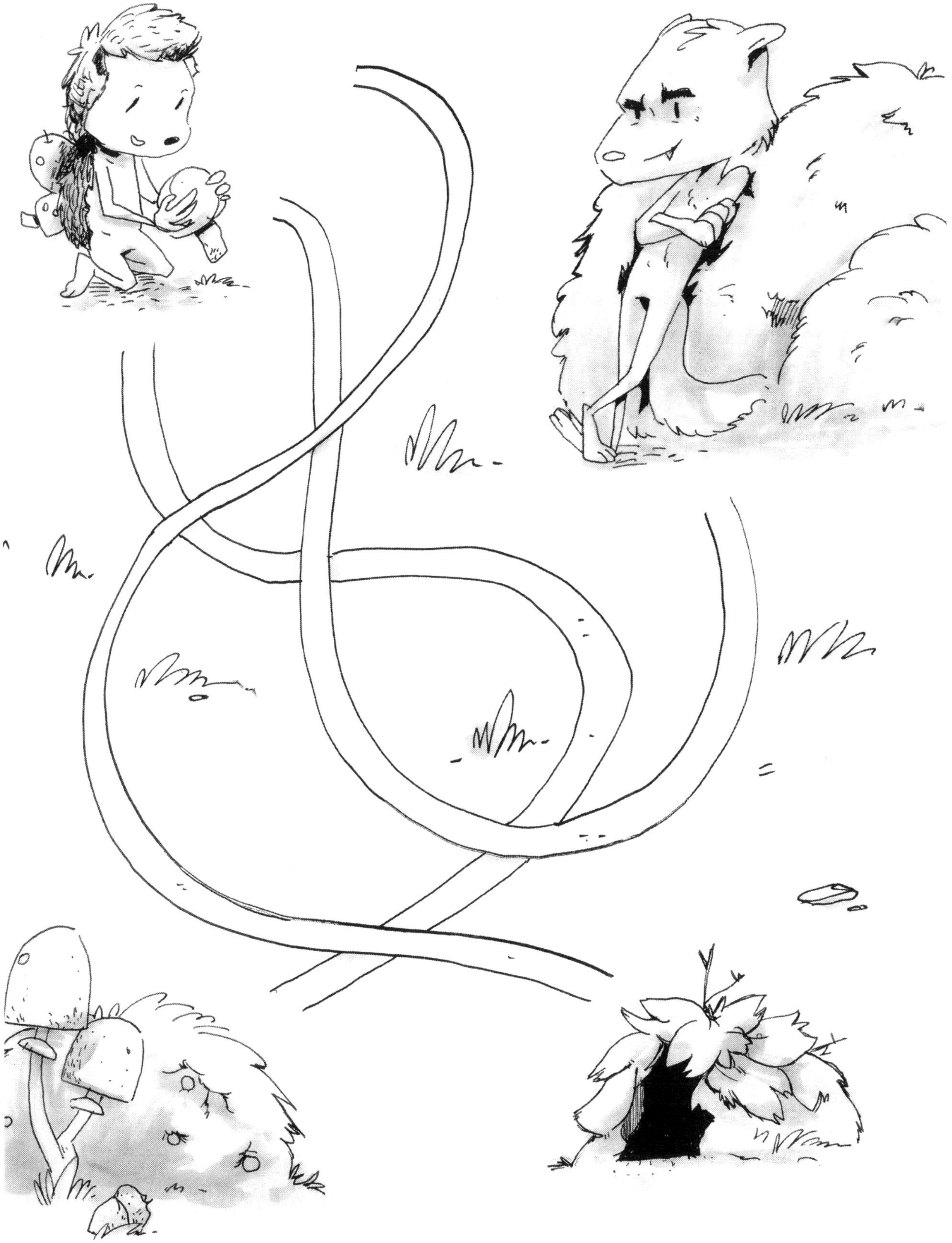

MOVIE TIME

Watch a movie or documentary about animals.

TITLE:_____

RATING

Draw Your Favorite Scenes:

A B C D E F G
H I J K L M
N O P Q R S T
U V W X Y Z

a b c d e f g h
i j k l m n o p
q r s t u v w x
y z 1 2 3 4 5 6 7 8 9 0

Today's Date:

TO-DO LIST

1._____

2._____

3._____

4._____

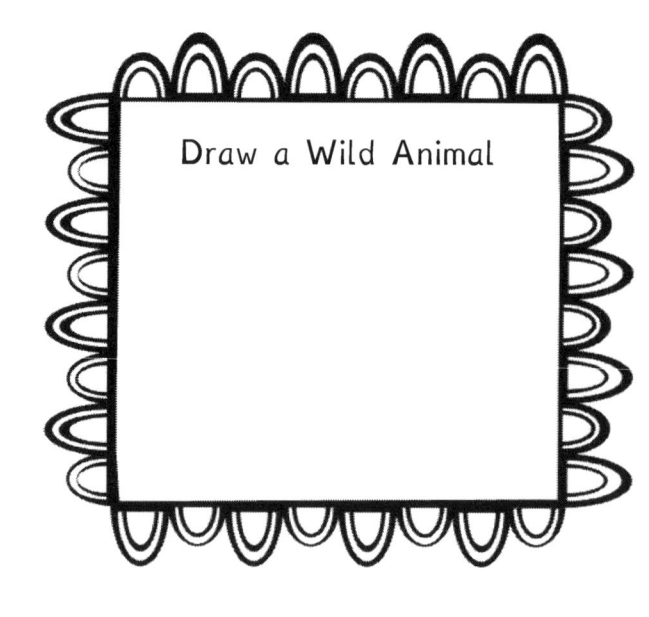

Draw a Wild Animal

How are you FEELING TODAY?

Draw a Pet

FIELD TRIPS & BACKYARD SCIENCE

Go somewhere and draw what you see! Look for animals!

If you can't go very far, go to a park or your own backyard.

Today's Date: _____

Today I Saw: _____
_____
_____

WHAT DID YOU LEARN ABOUT HISTORY TODAY?

WHAT DID YOU LEARN ABOUT SCIENCE TODAY?

WILDLIFE & GEOGRAPHY

RESEARCH AN ANIMAL OF YOUR CHOICE: _____

WHERE IN THE WORLD DOES THIS ANIMAL LIVE?

FUN FACTS:

DRAW THE ANIMAL:

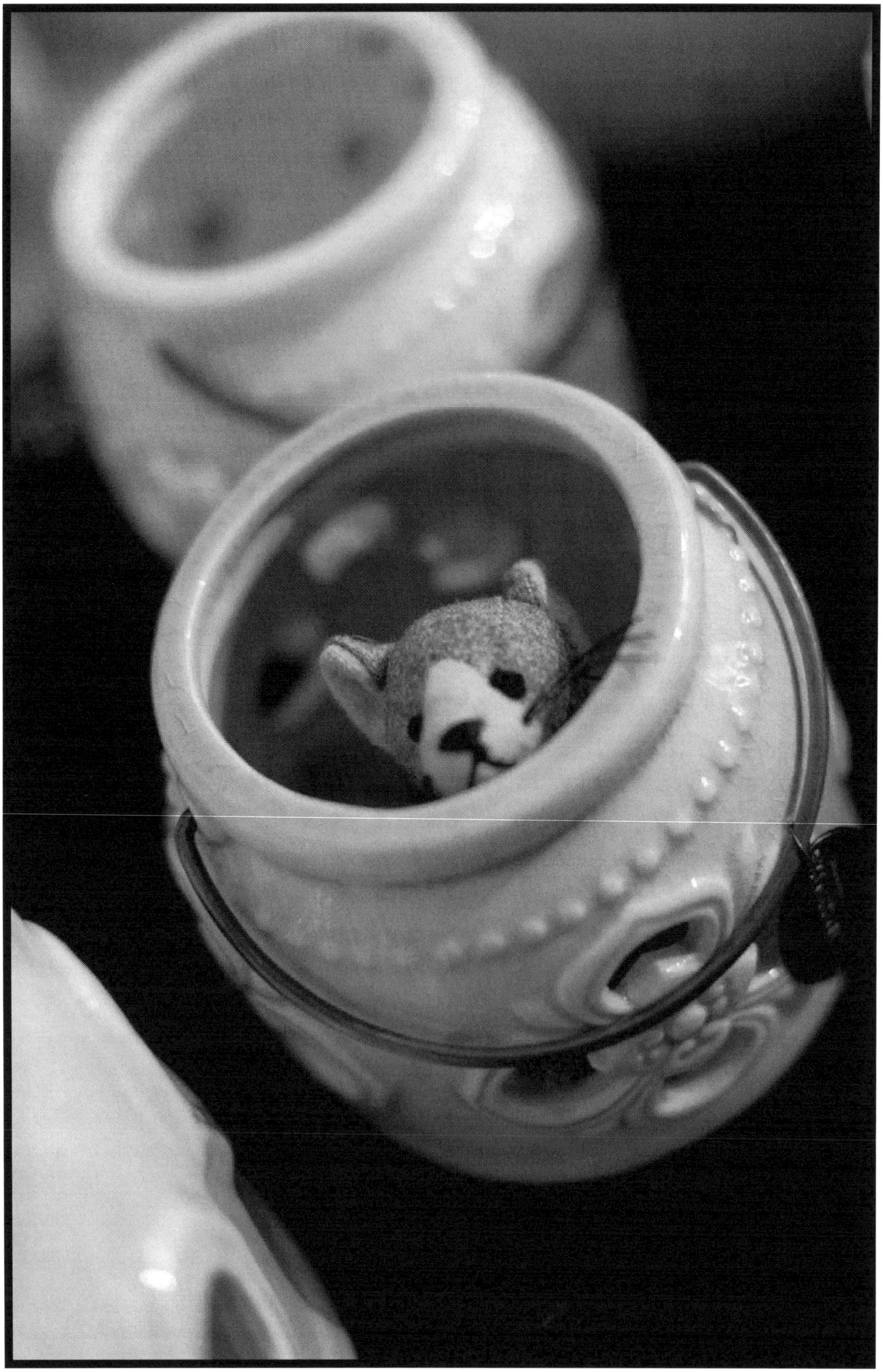

STORY WRITING TIME

If you can't think and write at the same time, record your story or ask someone older for help.

Title:

Names & Descriptions of Characters:

Base your story on the picture to the left.

Today's Date:

READING TIME

Write and draw about what you are reading.

COPYWORK

Copy a paragraph from one of your library books.

TITLE: _____ Page#_____

_____

_____

_____

_____

_____

DRAWING TIME

Copy an illustration from one of your books.

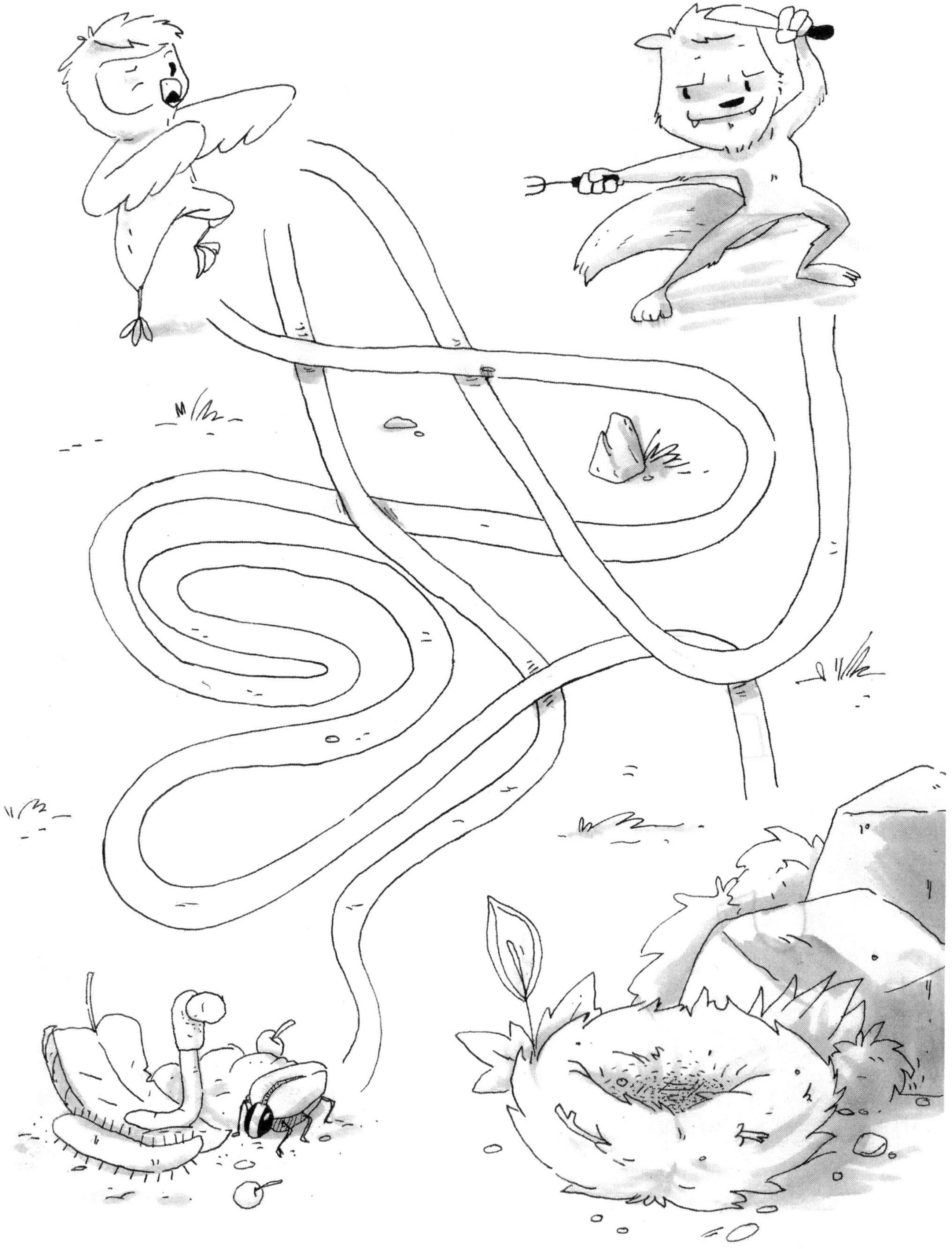

CURSIVE WRITING PRACTICE

A B C D E F G
H I J K L M
N O P Q R S T
U V W X Y Z

a b c d e f g h
i j k l m n o p
q r s t u v w x
y z 1 2 3 4 5 6 7 8 9 0

SPELLING TIME

Choose a Letter: ___

Find 15 words that begin or end with that letter.

Five Nouns:

_____
_____
_____
_____
_____

Five Adjectives:

_____
_____
_____
_____
_____

Three Animals:

_____
_____
_____

Two Verbs:

_____
_____

Write a silly story, poem, song or play using words from your spelling list.

_____
_____
_____
_____
_____
_____
_____
_____
_____
_____
_____
_____
_____
_____
_____
_____
_____

CREATE A COMIC STRIP

Use your spelling words.

SPELLING TIME

Choose an Animal

_____

Look in your books for 10 words that have some of the same letters as this animal.

1. _____
2. _____
3. _____
4. _____
5. _____
6. _____
7. _____
8. _____
9. _____
10. _____

CREATIVE WRITING

Write a short story about this picture. Ask someone older to help you write the words.

_____
_____
_____
_____
_____
_____
_____
_____

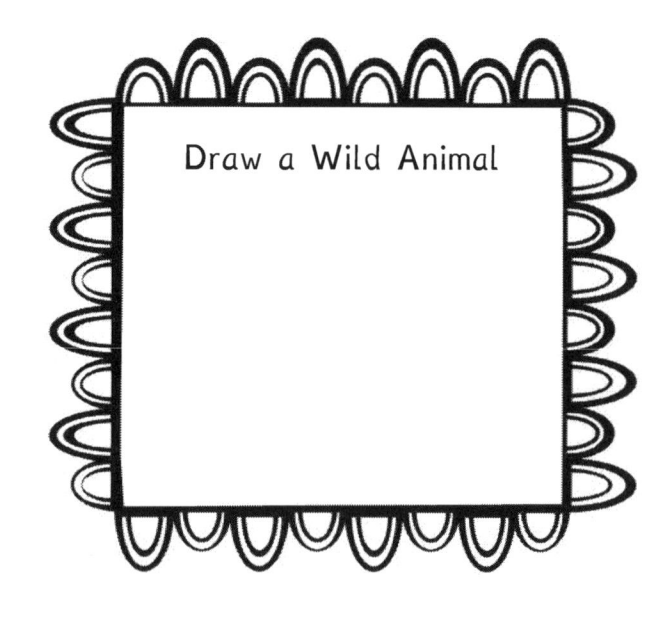

Today's Date:

TO-DO LIST

1._____

2._____

3._____

4._____

Draw a Wild Animal

How are you FEELING TODAY?

Draw a Pet

LISTENING TIME

CLASSICAL MUSIC & LITERATURE

Today's Date:_____

Listen to an audio book or classical music.

Draw and doodle below.

I am listening to: _____

Today's Date:
_____

READING TIME

Write and draw about what you are reading.

FIELD TRIPS & BACKYARD SCIENCE

Go somewhere and draw what you see! Look for animals!

If you can't go very far, go to a park or your own backyard.

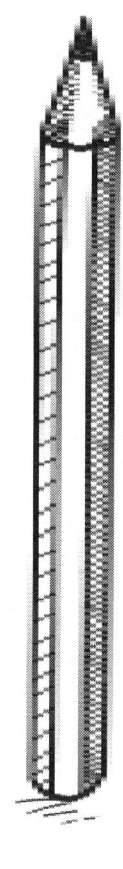

Today's Date: _____

Today I Saw: _____

_____

_____

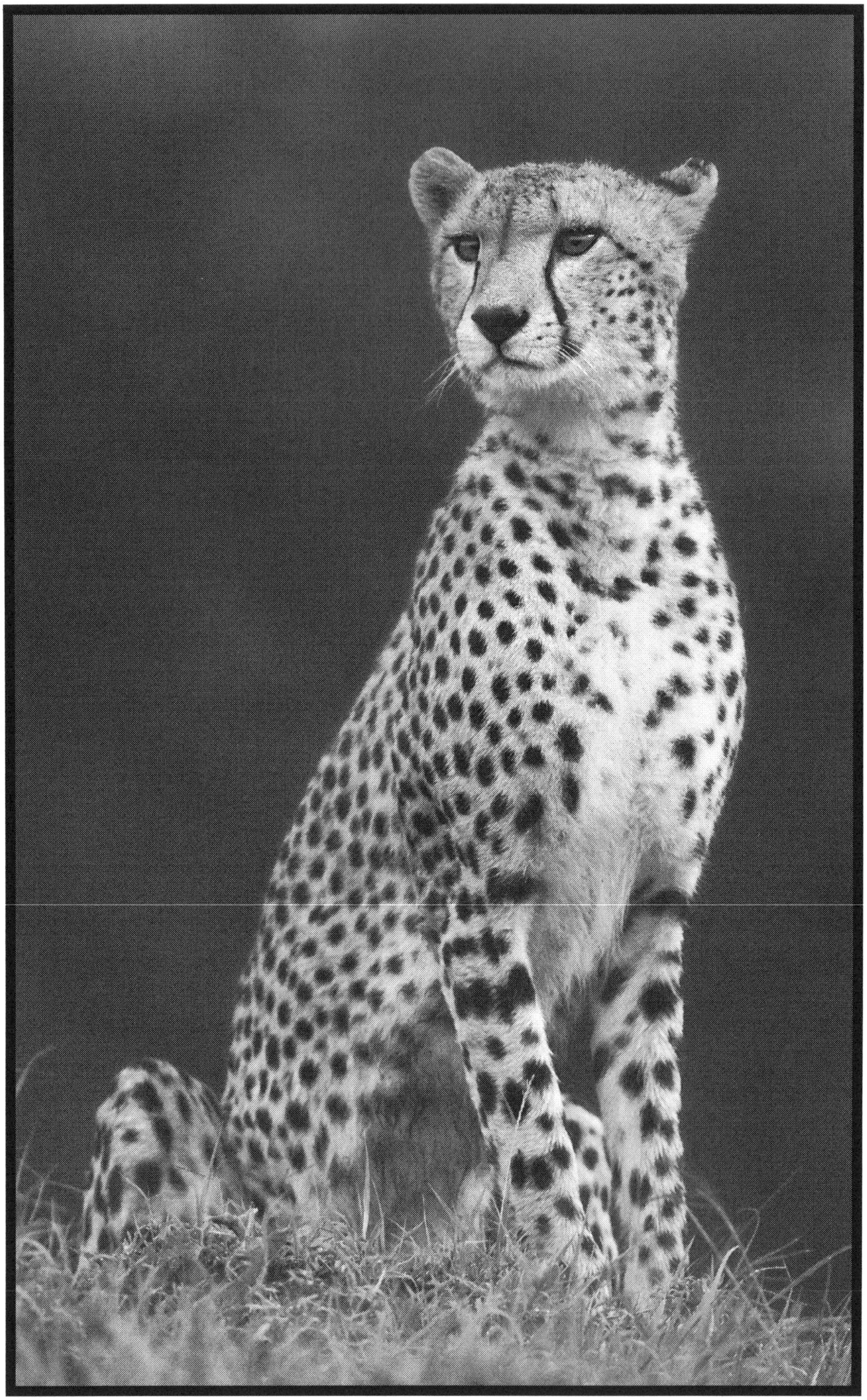

Trace & Color

Today's Date:

TO-DO LIST

1._____

2._____

3._____

4._____

ABCDEFG
HIJKLMN
OPQRSTU
VWXYZ

How are you FEELING TODAY?

Draw a Pet

ANIMAL QUIZ

I am _____

I live in _____

I like to eat _____

My enemies are _____

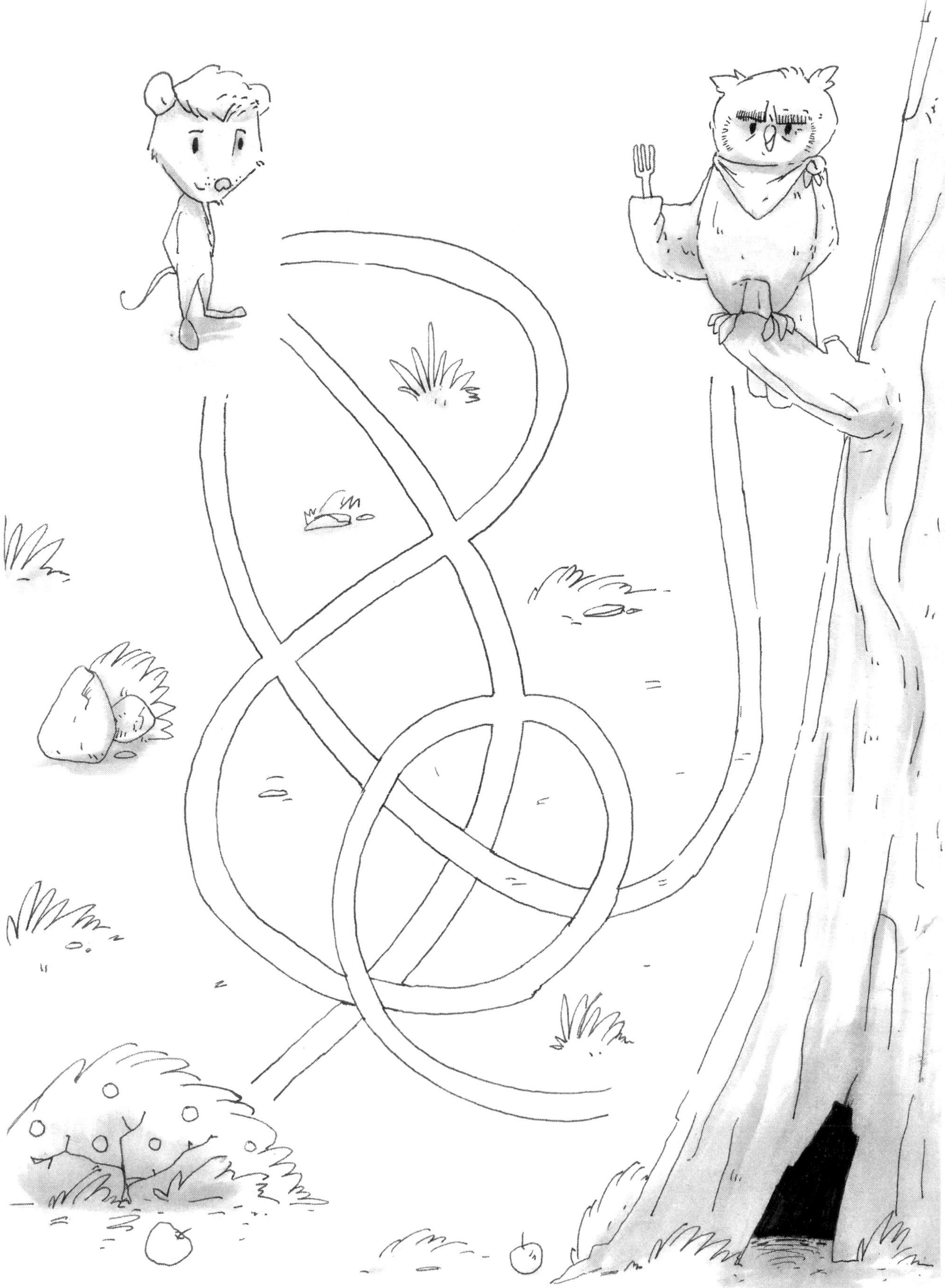

CREATIVE WRITING

Write a short story about this picture. Ask someone older to help you write the words.

_____
_____
_____
_____
_____
_____
_____
_____
_____

WHAT DID YOU LEARN ABOUT HISTORY TODAY?

WHAT DID YOU LEARN ABOUT SCIENCE TODAY?

WILDLIFE & GEOGRAPHY

RESEARCH AN ANIMAL OF YOUR CHOICE: _____

WHERE IN THE WORLD DOES THIS ANIMAL LIVE?

FUN FACTS:

DRAW THE ANIMAL:

MOVIE TIME

Watch a movie or documentary about animals.

TITLE:_____

RATING

Draw Your Favorite Scenes:

MATH & DESIGN TIME

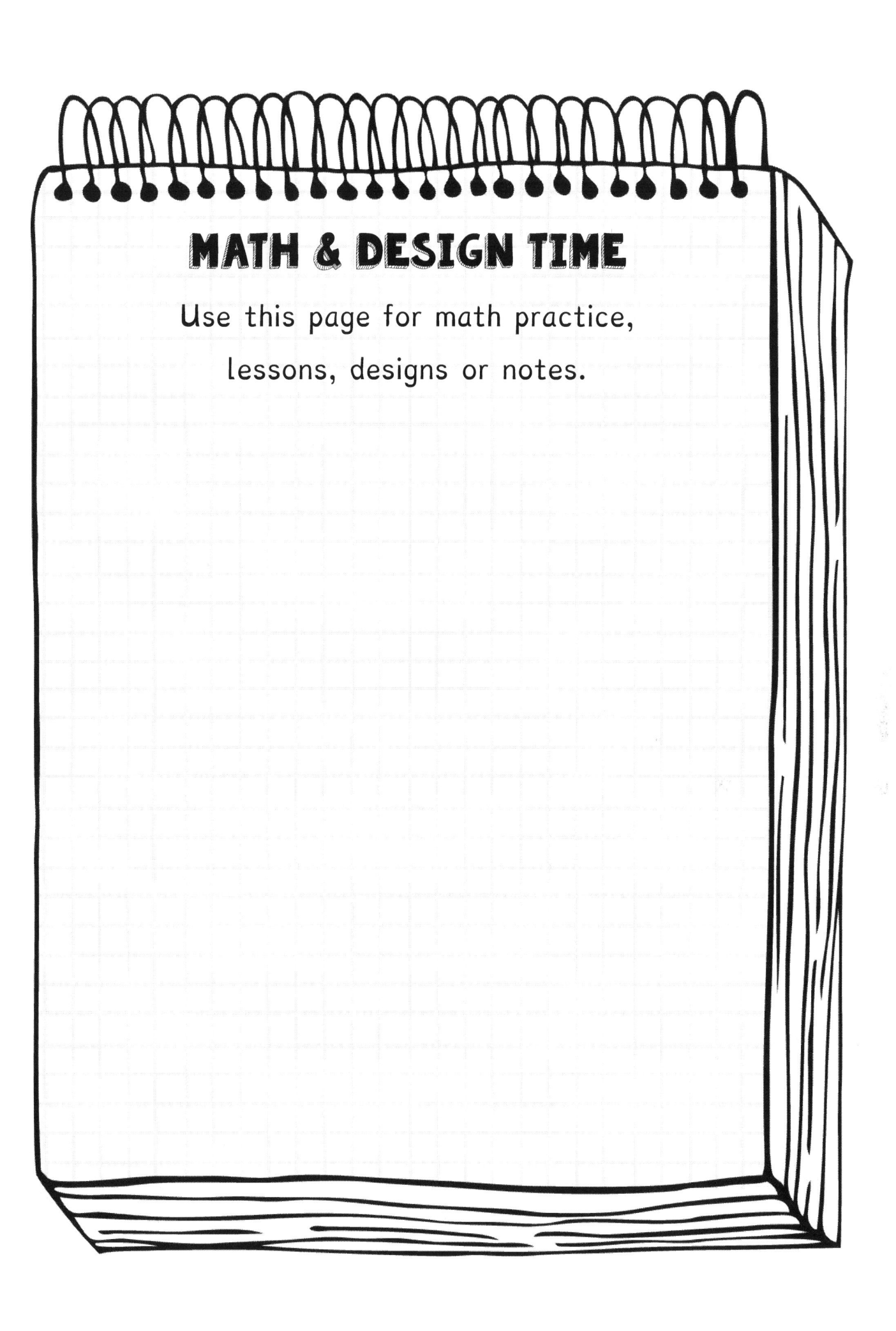

Use this page for math practice, lessons, designs or notes.

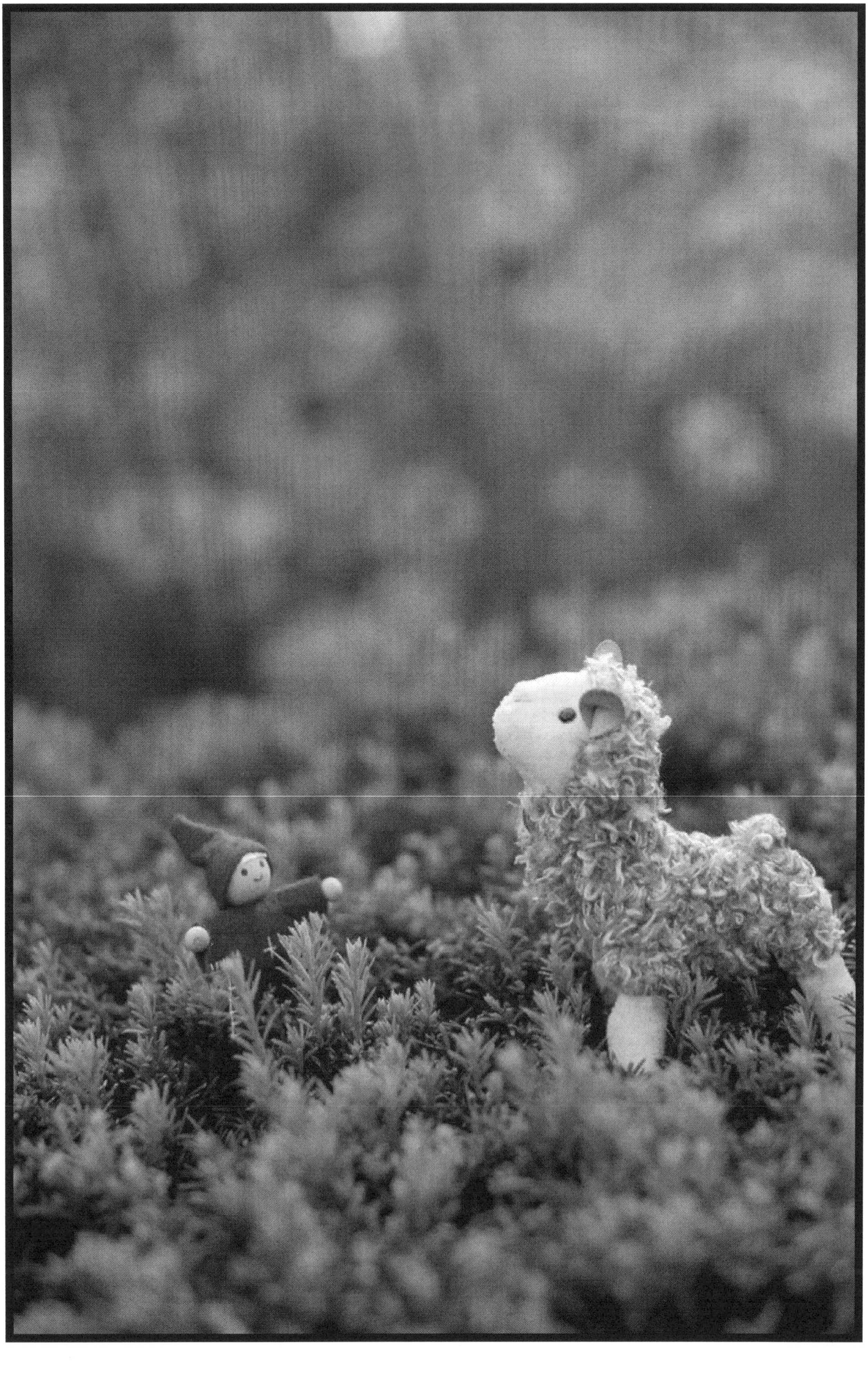

STORY WRITING TIME

If you can't think and write at the same time, record your story or ask someone older for help.

Title:

___

Names & Descriptions of Characters:

Base your story on the picture to the left.

SPELLING TIME

Choose a Letter: ___

Find 15 words that begin or end with that letter.

Five Nouns:

_____
_____
_____
_____
_____

Five Adjectives:

_____
_____
_____
_____
_____

Three Animals:

_____
_____
_____

Two Verbs:

_____
_____

Write a silly story, poem, song or play using words from your spelling list.

_____
_____
_____
_____
_____
_____
_____
_____
_____
_____
_____
_____
_____
_____
_____
_____
_____
_____

CREATE A COMIC STRIP

Use your spelling words.

Today's Date:
_____

READING TIME

Write and draw about what you are reading.

ORIGAMI CHALLENGE
CAN YOU MAKE THIS ANIMAL?

Set a timer.

Minutes:_____   Seconds:_____

An Asian racoon

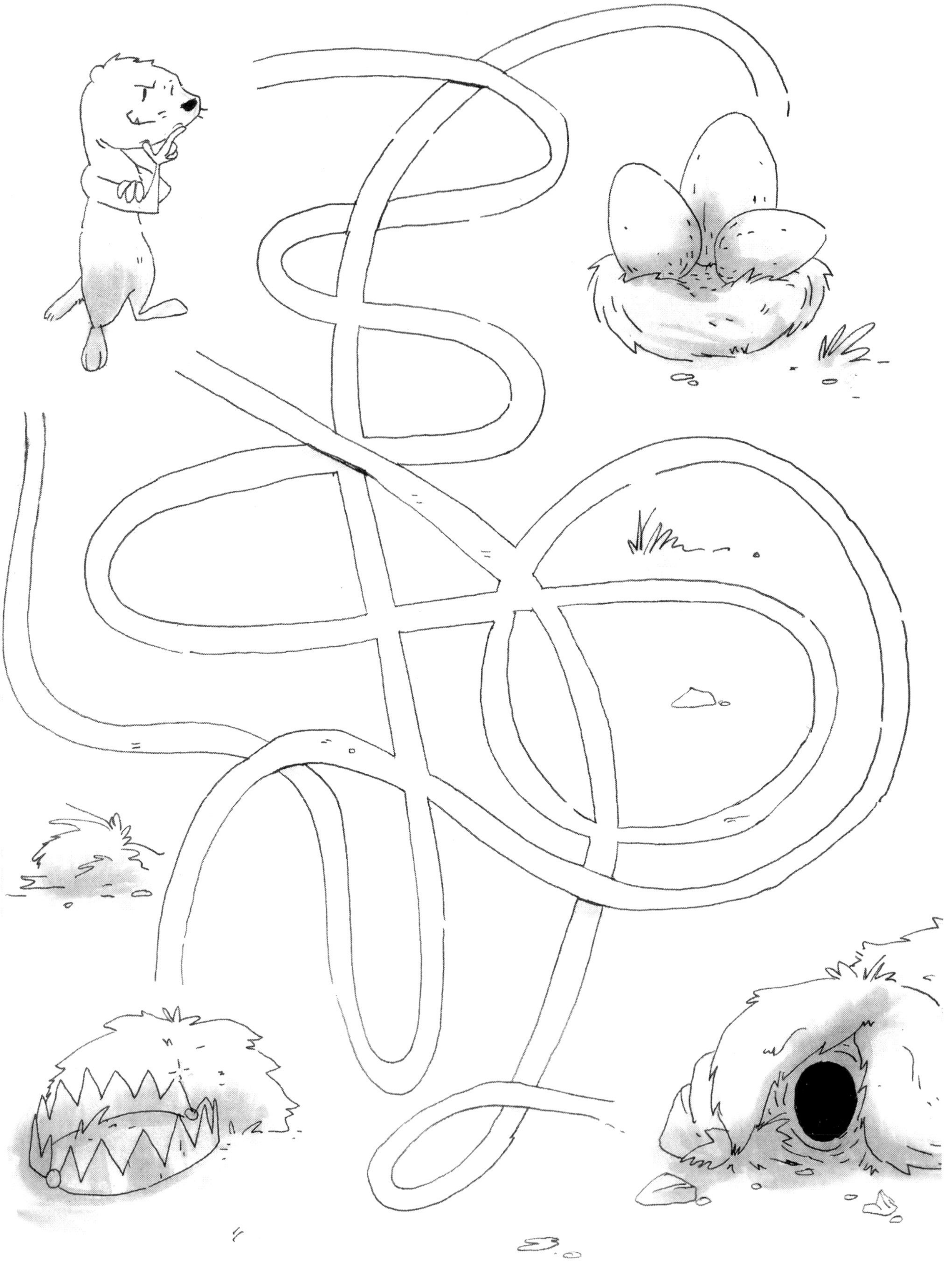

DRAW MY HABITAT

Today's Date:

TO-DO LIST

1._____

2._____

3._____

4._____

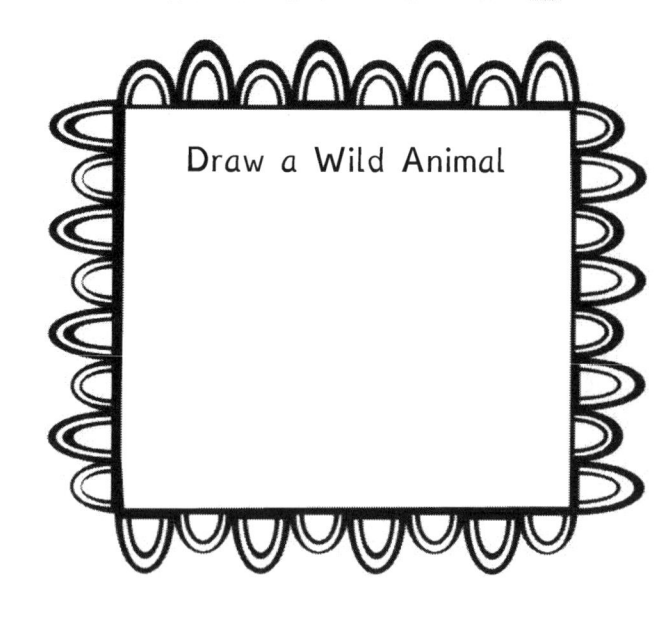

Draw a Wild Animal

How are you FEELING TODAY?

Draw a Pet

DRAW MY HABITAT

Today's Date:

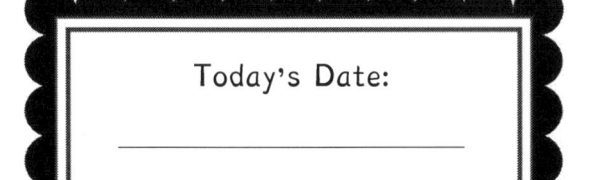

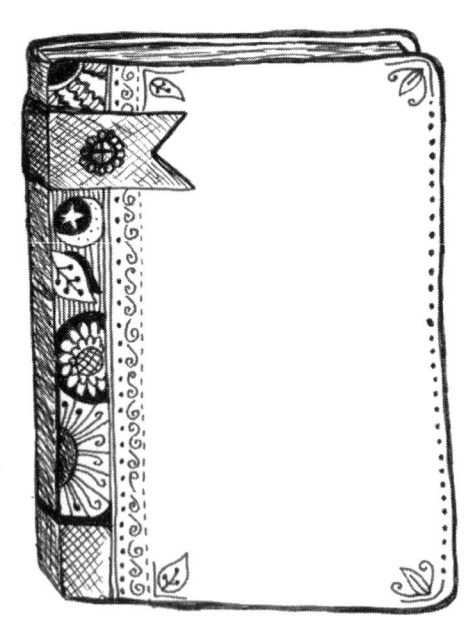

READING TIME

Write and draw about what you are reading.

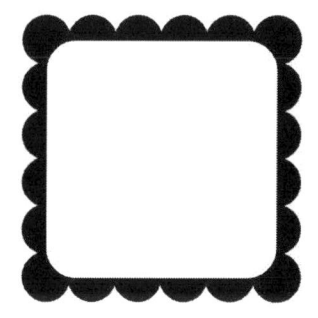

FIELD TRIPS & BACKYARD SCIENCE

Go somewhere and draw what you see! Look for animals!

If you can't go very far, go to a park or your own backyard.

Today's Date: _____

Today I Saw: _____

_____

_____

SPELLING TIME

Choose an Animal

_____

Look in your books for 10 words that have some of the same letters as this animal.

1. _____
2. _____
3. _____
4. _____
5. _____
6. _____
7. _____
8. _____
9. _____
10. _____

ANIMAL QUIZ

I am _____

I live in _____

I like to eat _____

My enemies are _____

MOVIE TIME

Watch a movie or documentary about animals.

TITLE:_____

Draw Your Favorite Scenes:

RATING

CURSIVE WRITING PRACTICE

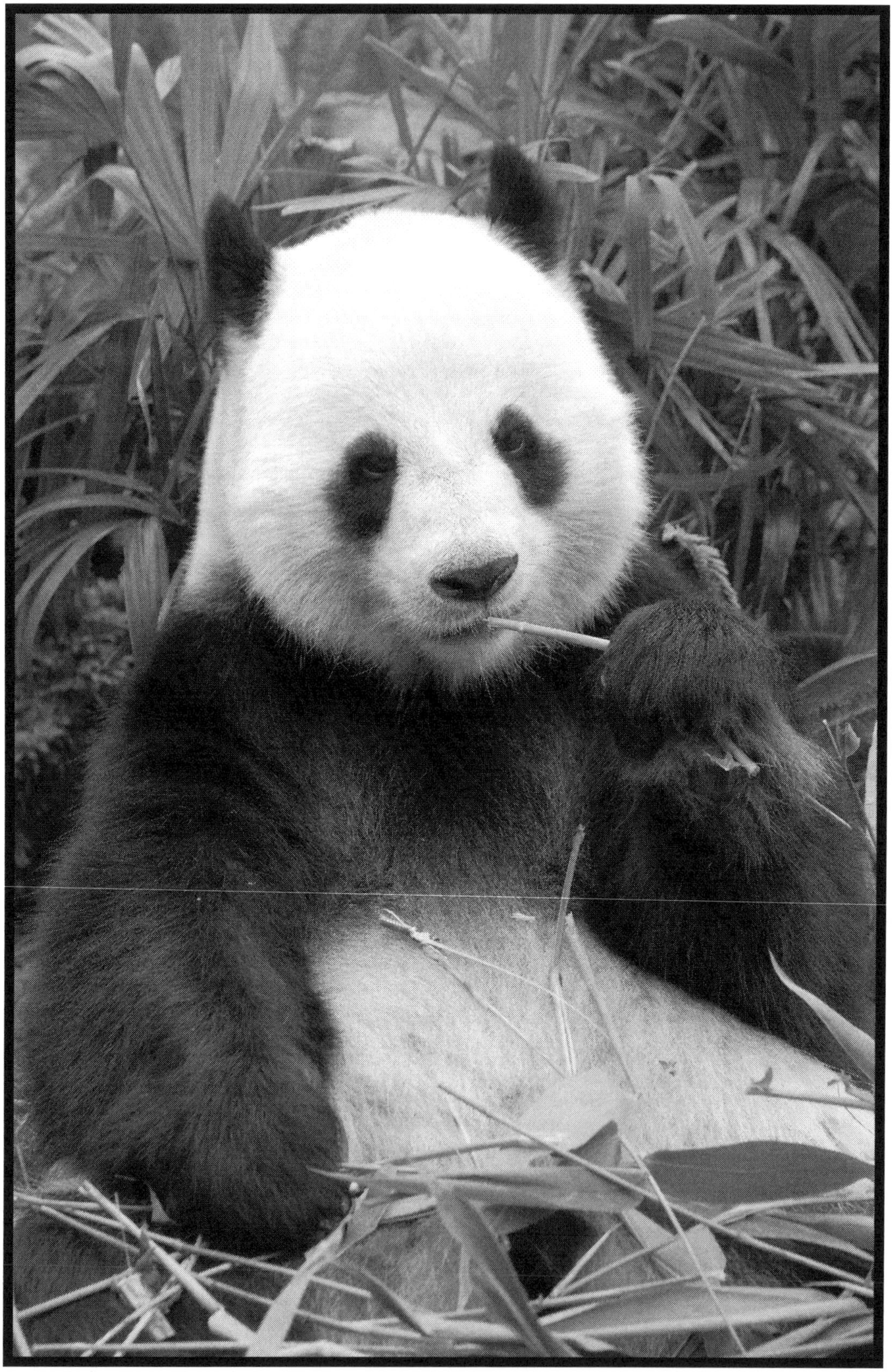

Trace & Color

WHAT DID YOU LEARN ABOUT HISTORY TODAY?

WHAT DID YOU LEARN ABOUT SCIENCE TODAY?

WILDLIFE & GEOGRAPHY

RESEARCH AN ANIMAL OF YOUR CHOICE: _____

WHERE IN THE WORLD DOES THIS ANIMAL LIVE?

FUN FACTS:

DRAW THE ANIMAL:

Today's Date:

TO-DO LIST

1._____

2._____

3._____

4._____

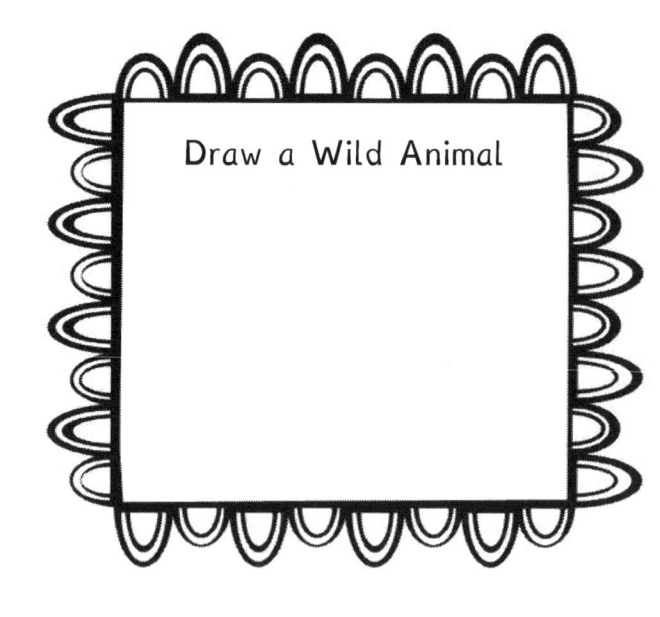

Draw a Wild Animal

How are you FEELING TODAY?

Draw a Pet

FIELD TRIPS & BACKYARD SCIENCE

Go somewhere and draw what you see! Look for animals!

If you can't go very far, go to a park or your own backyard.

Today's Date: _____

Today I Saw: _____

_____

_____

SPELLING TIME

Choose a Letter: ___

Find 15 words that begin or end with that letter.

Five Nouns:

_____
_____
_____
_____
_____

Five Adjectives:

_____
_____
_____
_____
_____

Three Animals:

_____
_____
_____

Two Verbs:

_____
_____

Write a silly story, poem, song or play using words from your spelling list.

_____
_____
_____
_____
_____
_____
_____
_____
_____
_____
_____
_____
_____
_____
_____
_____
_____
_____

CREATE A COMIC STRIP

Use your spelling words.

Today's Date:
_____

READING TIME

Write and draw about what you are reading.

COPYWORK

Copy a paragraph from one of your library books.

TITLE: _____ Page#_____

_____

_____

_____

_____

_____

DRAWING TIME

Copy an illustration from one of your books.

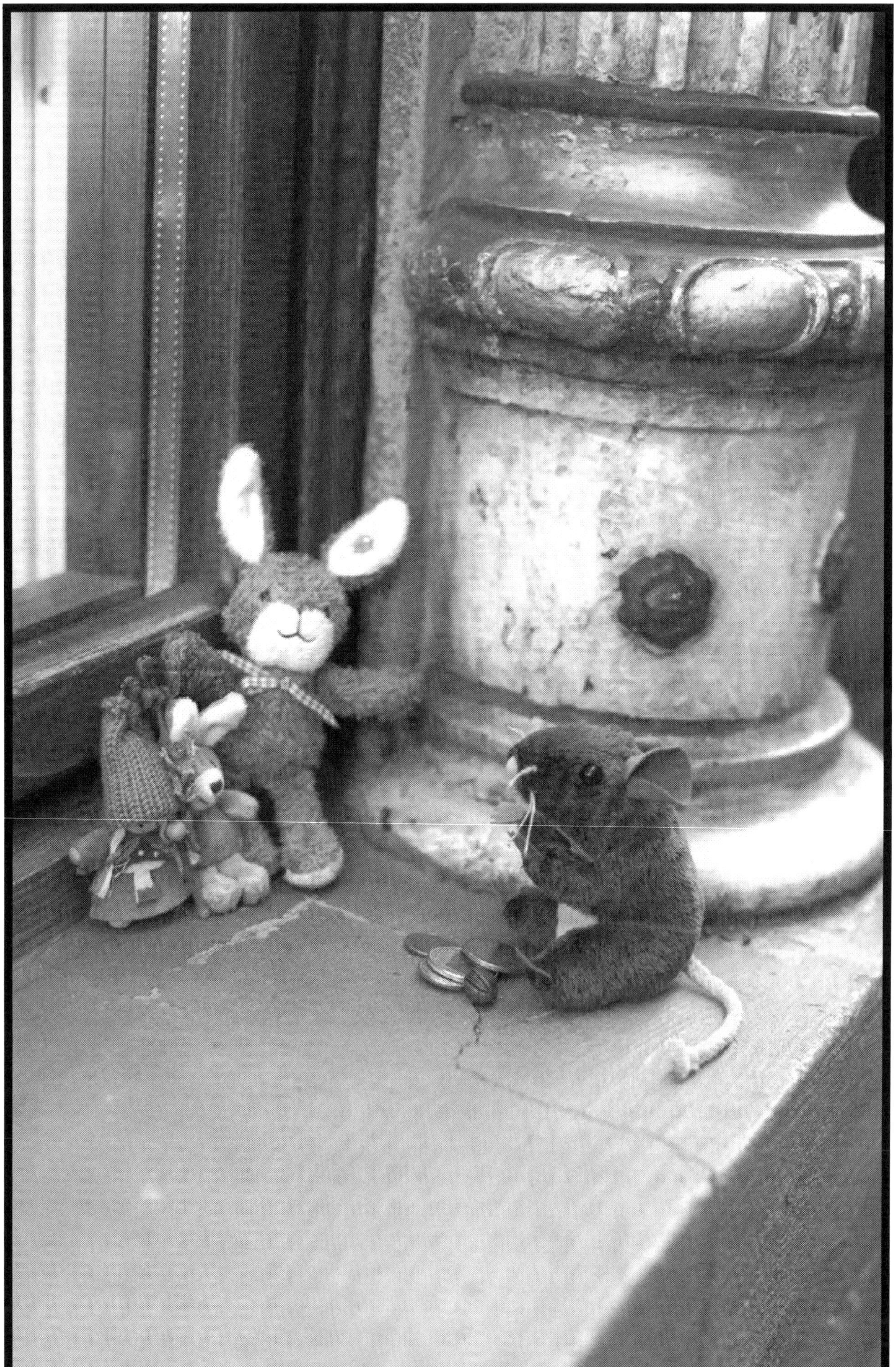

STORY WRITING TIME

If you can't think and write at the same time, record your story or ask someone older for help.

Title:

_____

Names & Descriptions of Characters:

_____
_____
_____
_____
_____
_____

Base your story on the picture to the left.

_____
_____
_____
_____
_____
_____
_____
_____
_____
_____
_____
_____
_____
_____
_____
_____

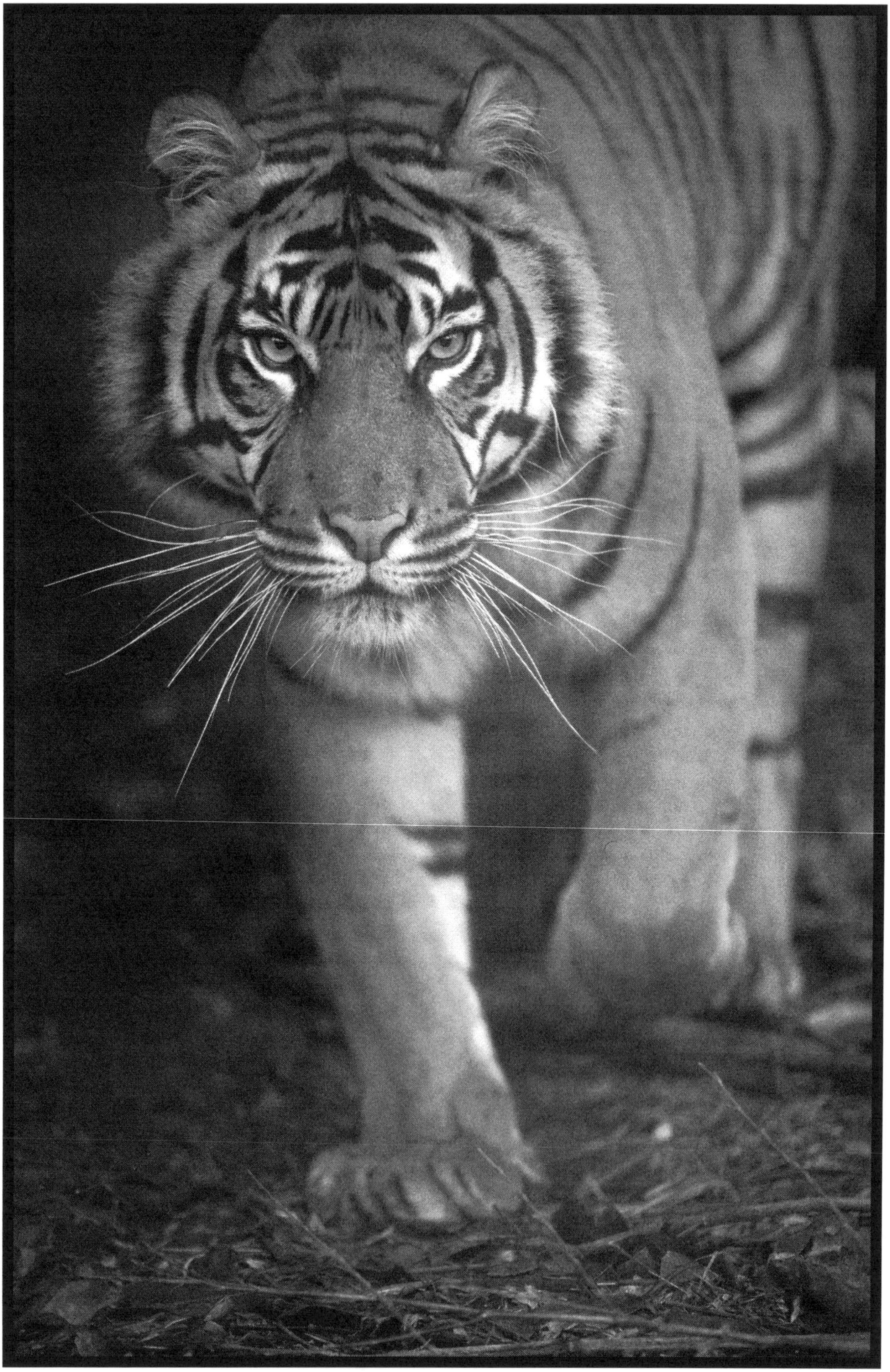

MATH & DESIGN TIME

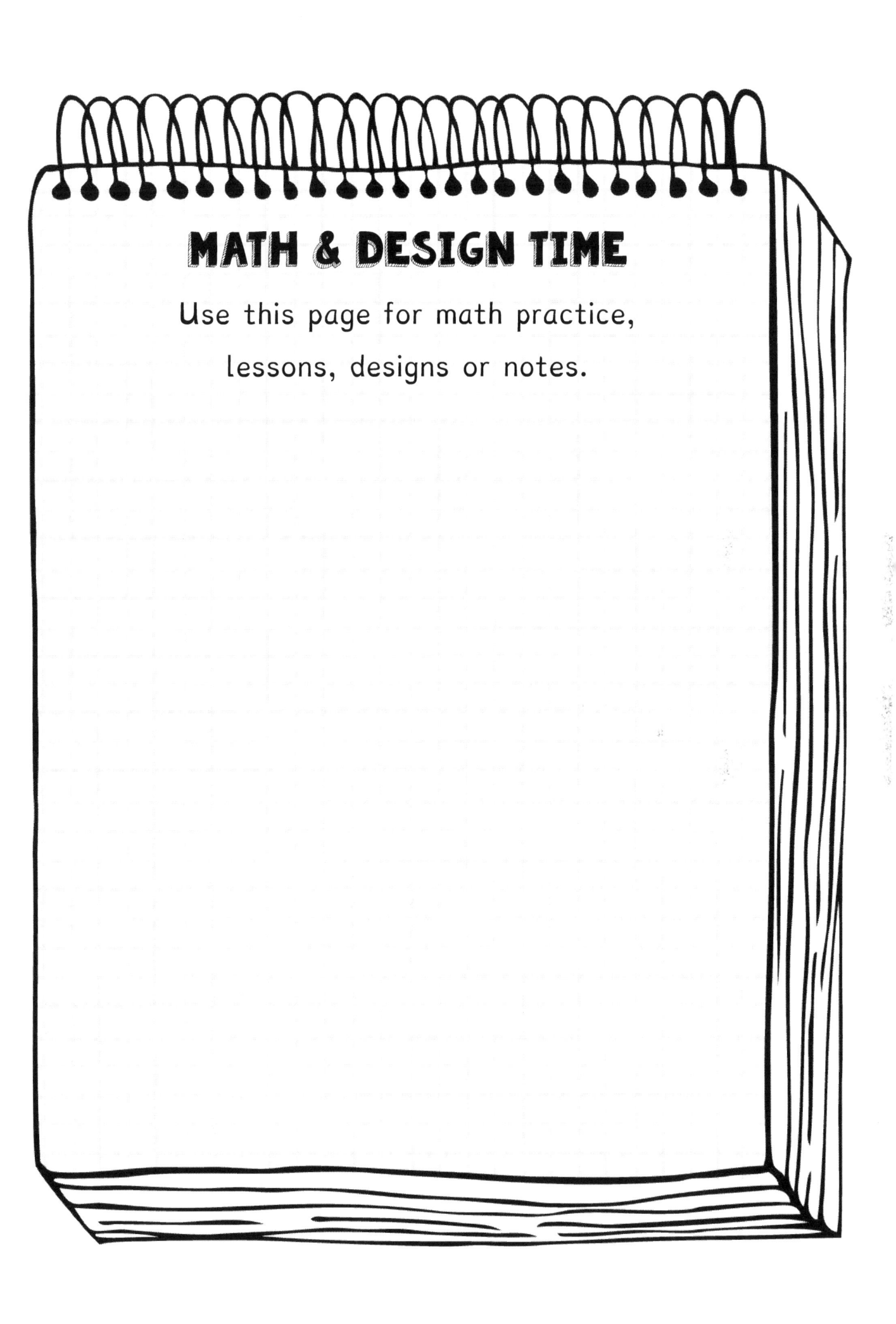

Use this page for math practice, lessons, designs or notes.

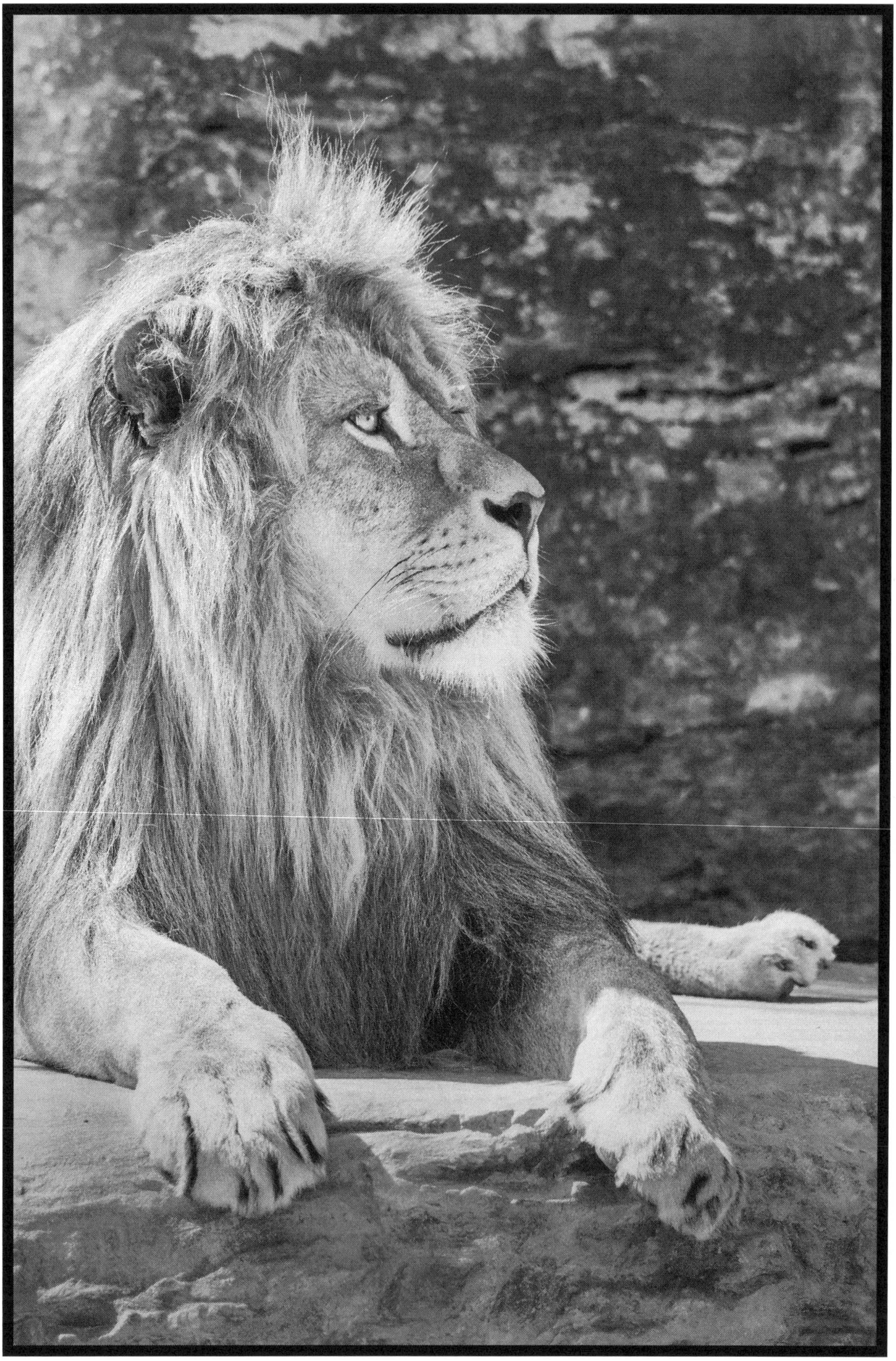

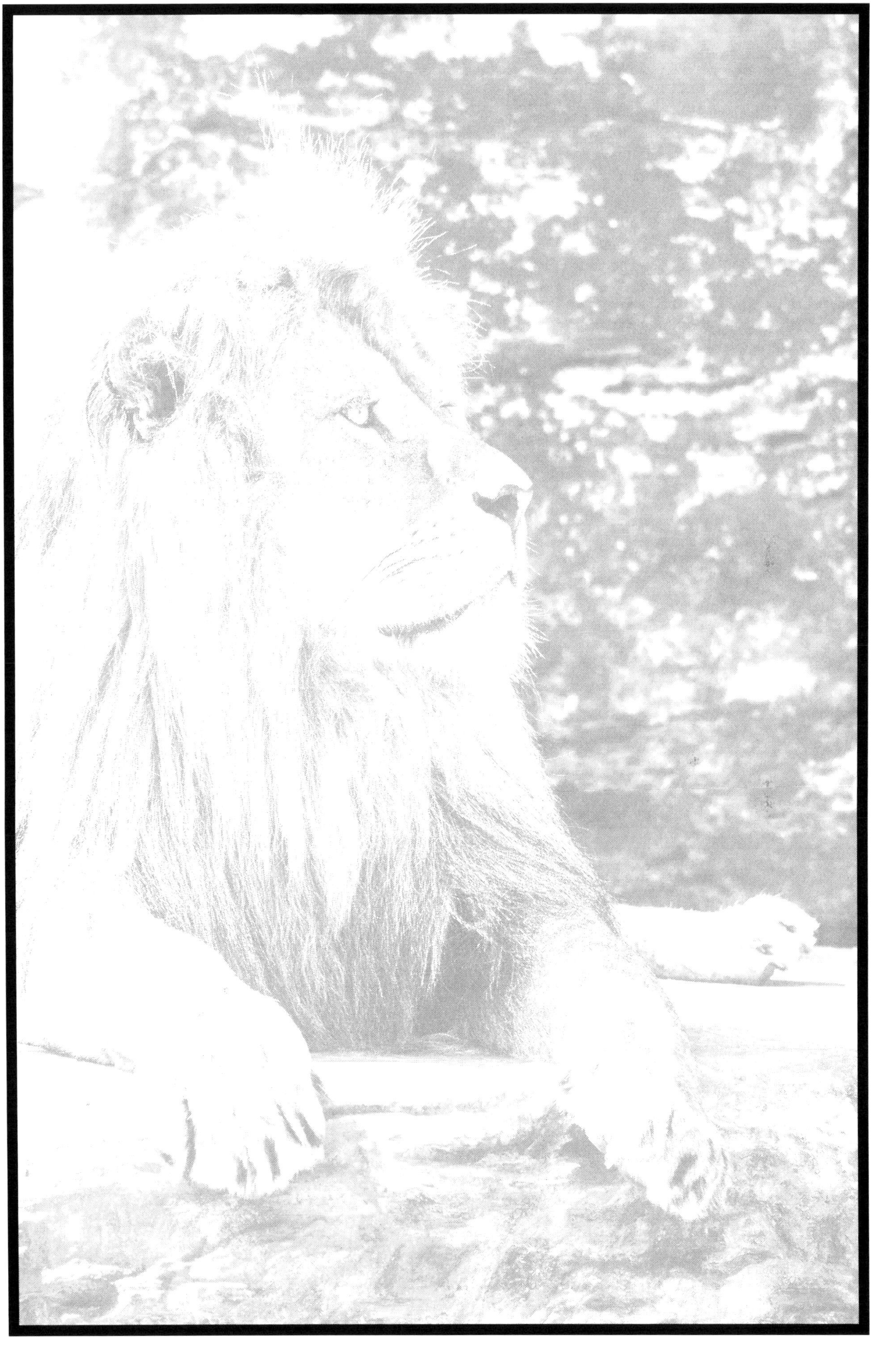

Today's Date:

TO-DO LIST

1._____
2._____
3._____
4._____

How are you FEELING TODAY?

Draw a Wild Animal

Draw a Pet

LISTENING TIME

CLASSICAL MUSIC & LITERATURE

Today's Date:_____

Listen to an audio book or classical music.

Draw and doodle below.

I am listening to: _____

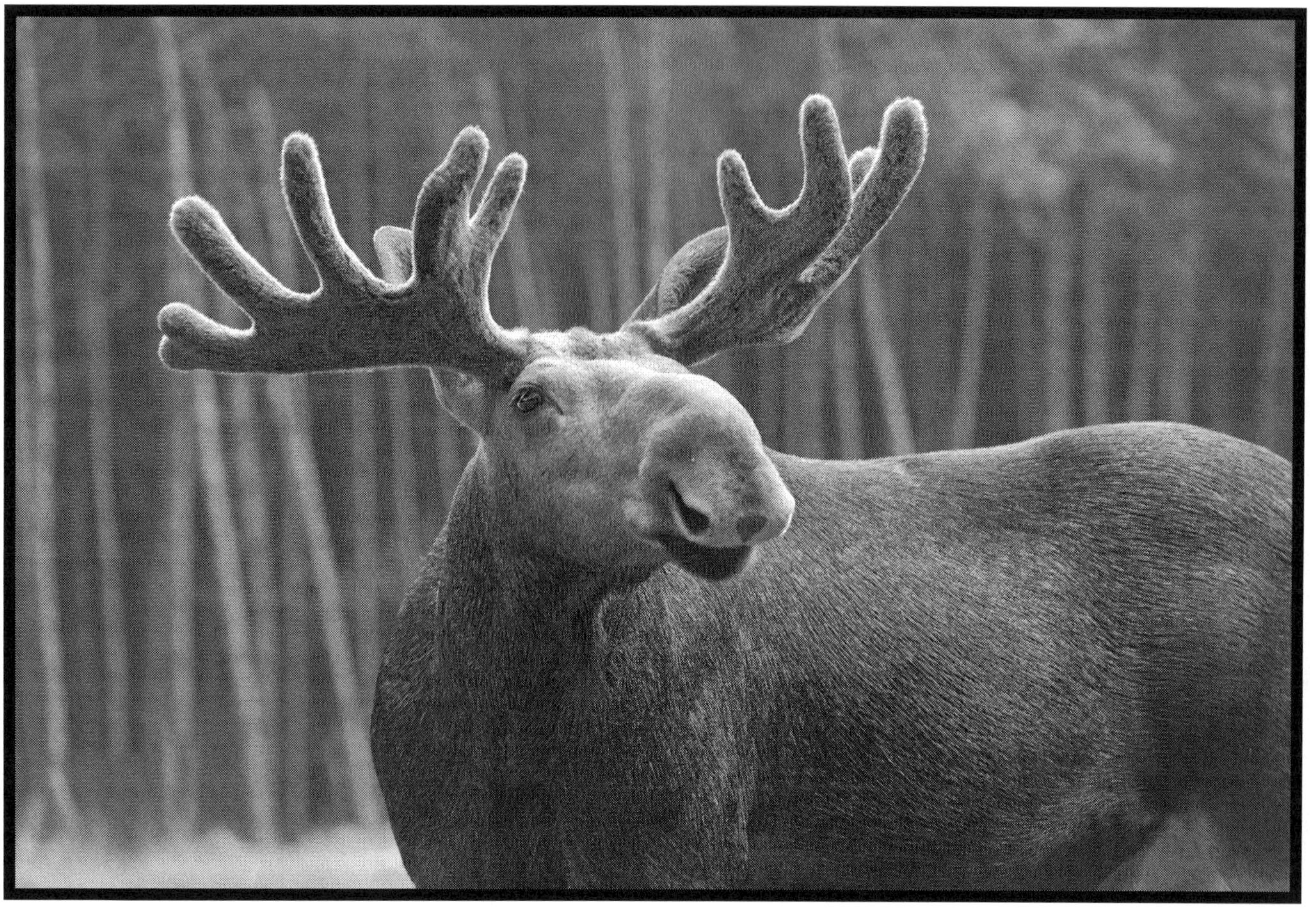

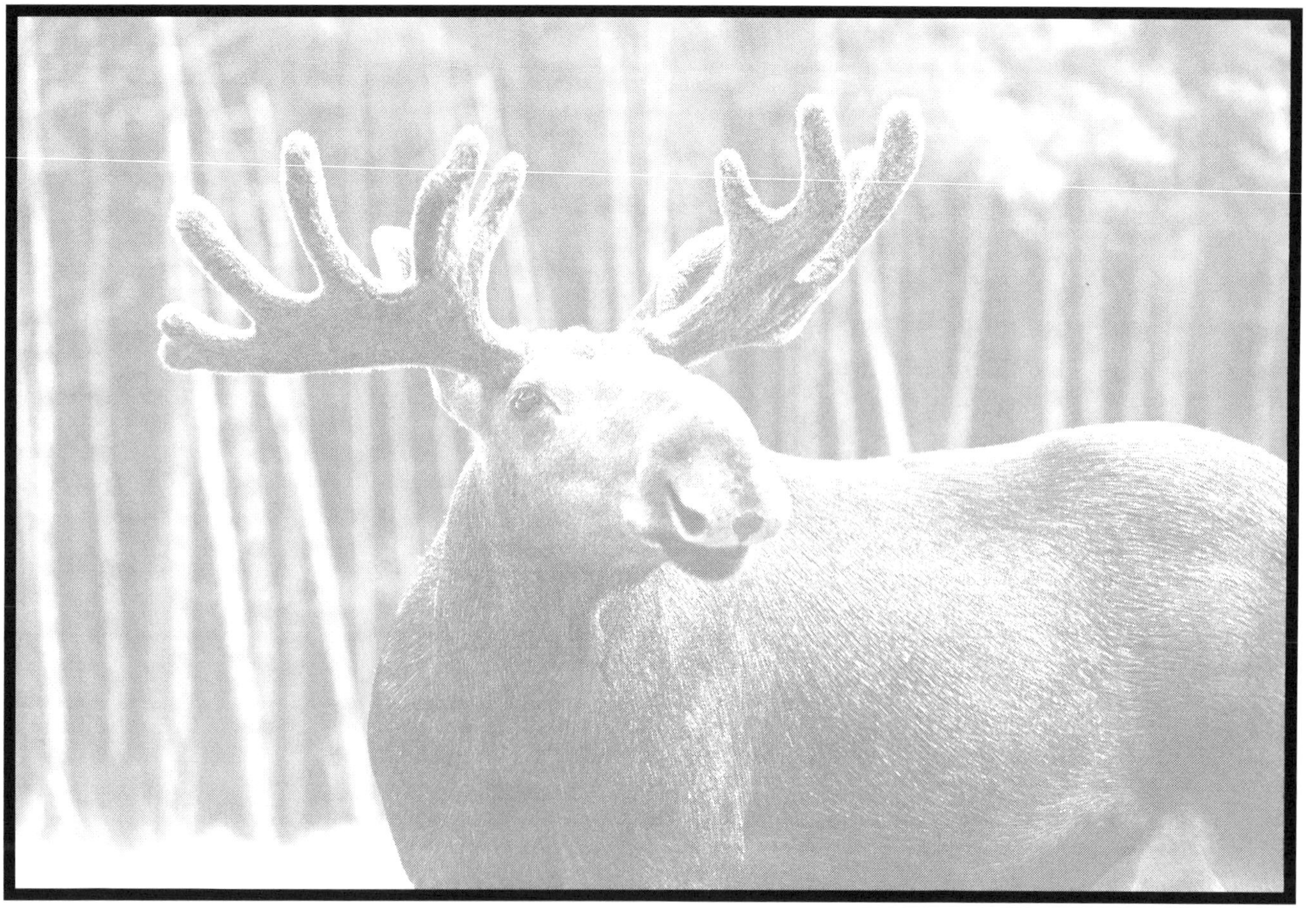

CURSIVE WRITING PRACTICE

A B C D E F G
H I J K L M
N O P Q R S T
U V W X Y Z

a b c d e f g h
i j k l m n o p
q r s t u v w x
y z 1 2 3 4 5 6 7 8 9 0

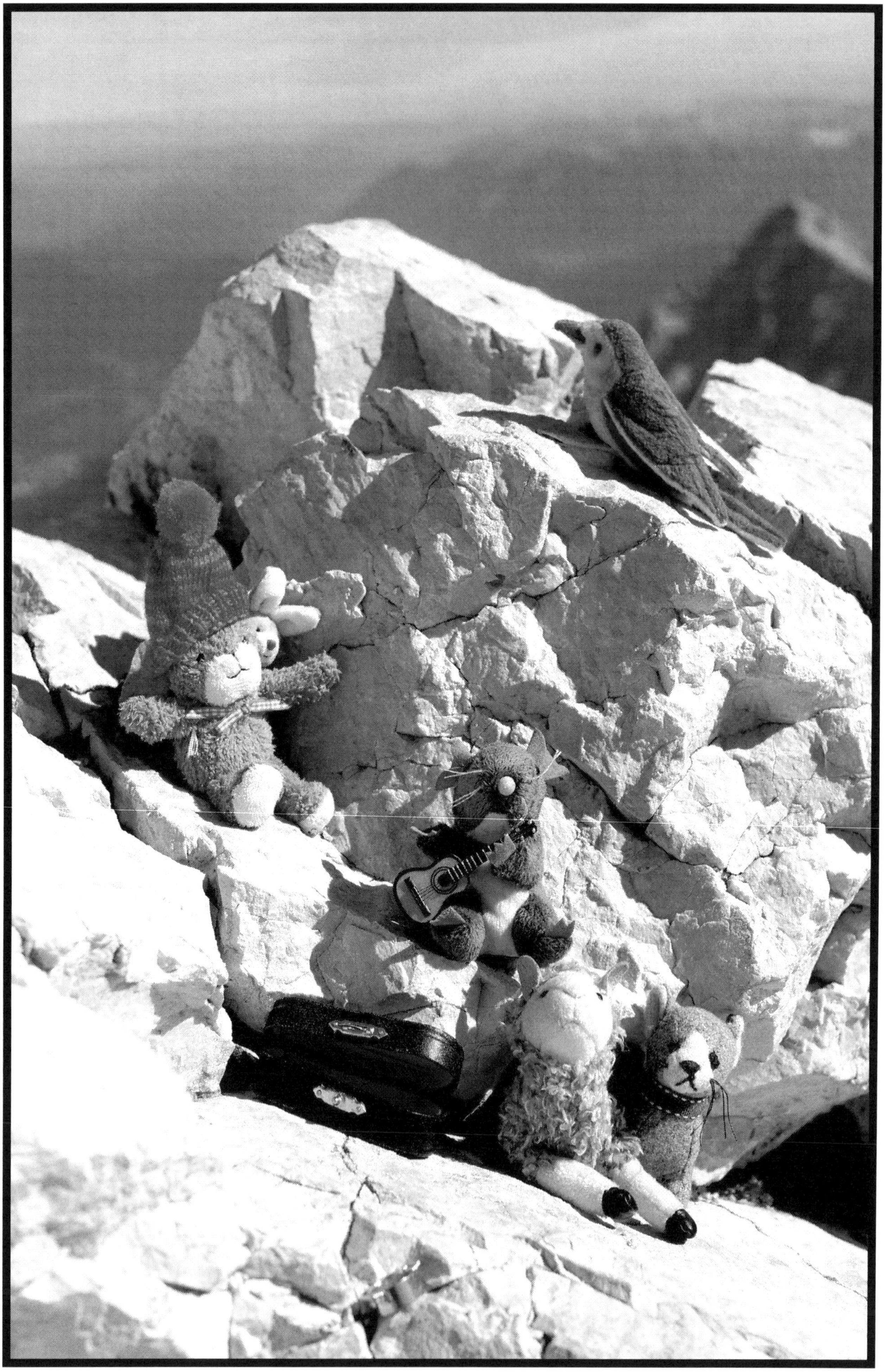

STORY WRITING TIME

If you can't think and write at the same time, record your story or ask someone older for help.

Title:

_____

Names & Descriptions of Characters:

_____
_____
_____
_____
_____

Base your story on the picture to the left.

_____
_____
_____
_____
_____
_____
_____
_____
_____
_____
_____
_____
_____
_____
_____
_____
_____

Today's Date:
_____

READING TIME

Write and draw about what you are reading.

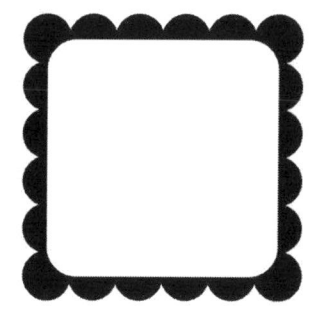

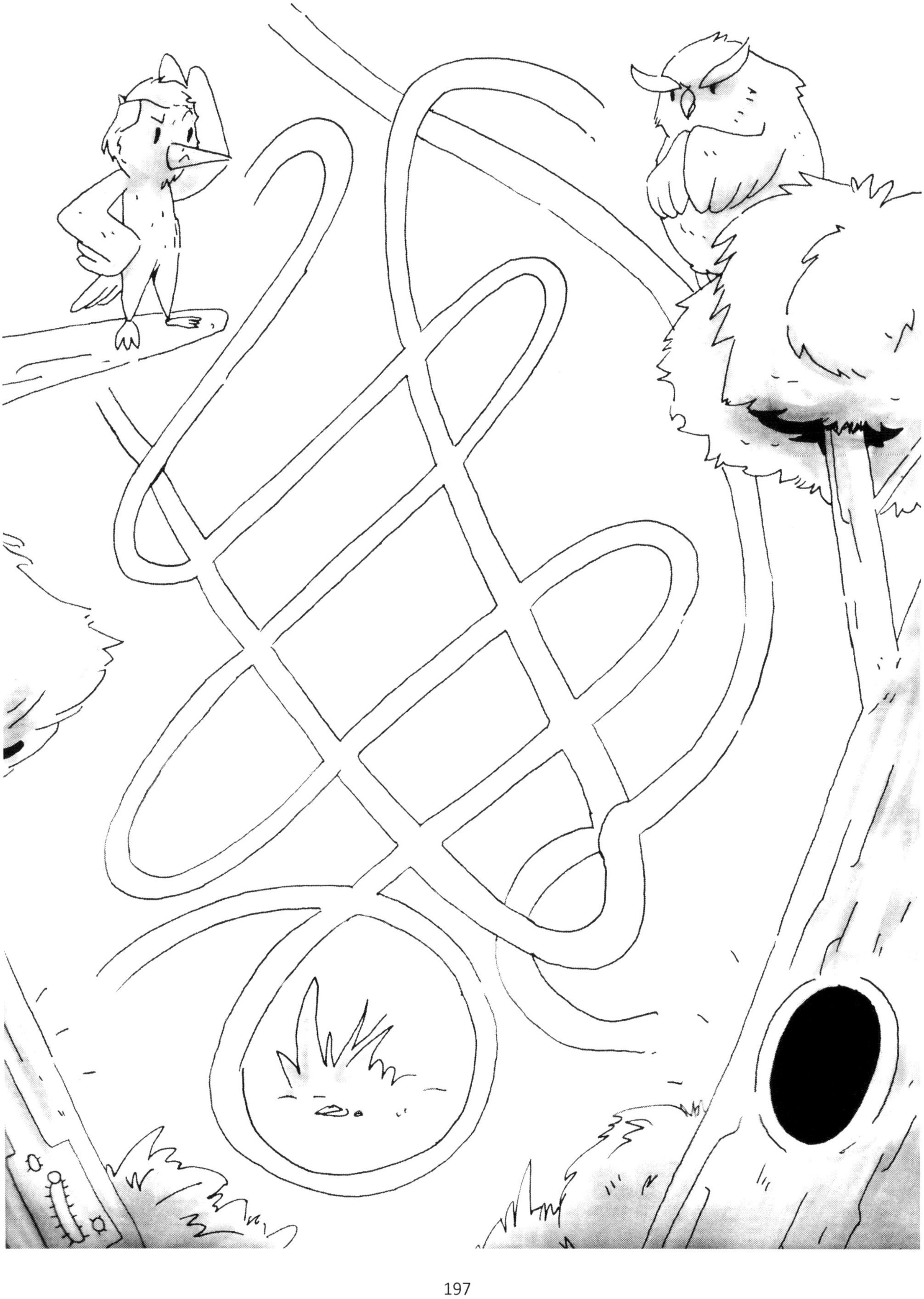

WHAT DID YOU LEARN ABOUT HISTORY TODAY?

WHAT DID YOU LEARN ABOUT SCIENCE TODAY?

WILDLIFE & GEOGRAPHY

RESEARCH AN ANIMAL OF YOUR CHOICE: _____

WHERE IN THE WORLD DOES THIS ANIMAL LIVE?

FUN FACTS:

DRAW THE ANIMAL:

SPELLING TIME

Choose a Letter: ___

Find 15 words that begin or end with that letter.

Five Nouns:
_____
_____
_____
_____
_____

Five Adjectives:
_____
_____
_____
_____
_____

Three Animals:
_____
_____
_____

Two Verbs:
_____
_____

Write a silly story, poem, song or play using words from your spelling list.

_____
_____
_____
_____
_____
_____
_____
_____
_____
_____
_____
_____
_____
_____
_____
_____
_____

CREATE A COMIC STRIP

Use your spelling words.

LISTENING TIME

CLASSICAL MUSIC & LITERATURE

Today's Date:_____

Listen to an audio book or classical music.

Draw and doodle below.

I am listening to: _____

DRAW MY HABITAT

MOVIE TIME

Watch a movie or documentary about animals.

TITLE:_____

RATING

Draw Your Favorite Scenes:

MATH & DESIGN TIME

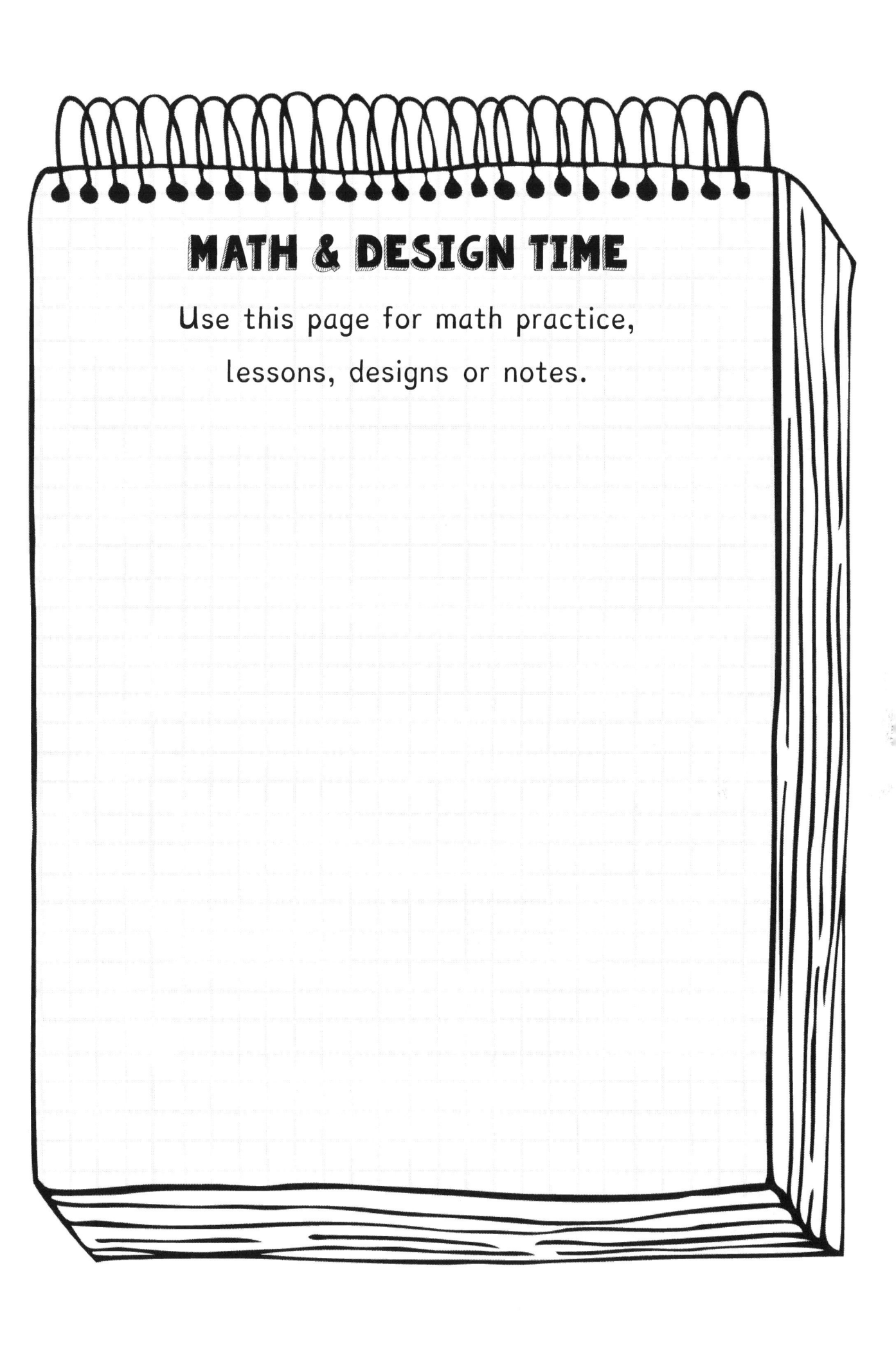

Use this page for math practice, lessons, designs or notes.

Today's Date:

TO-DO LIST

1._____

2._____

3._____

4._____

ABCDEFG
HIJKLMN
OPQRSTU
VWXYZ

How are you FEELING TODAY?

Draw a Pet

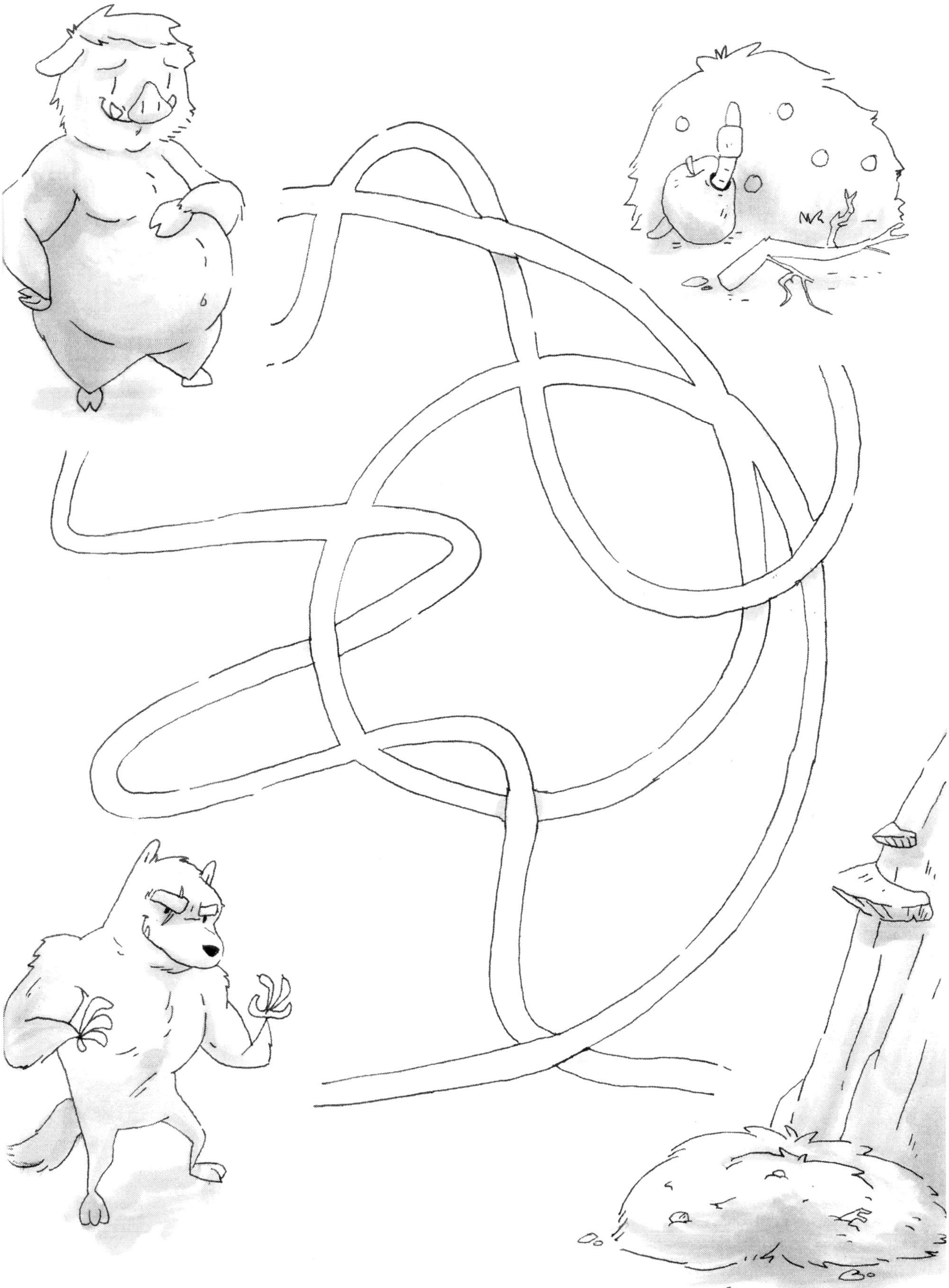

Today's Date:
_____

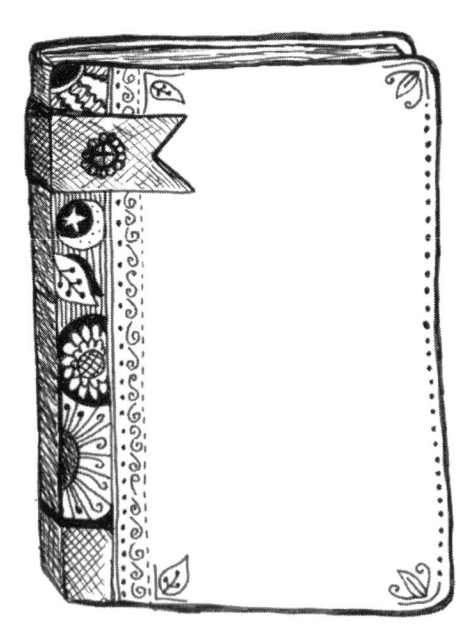

READING TIME

Write and draw about what you are reading.

FIELD TRIPS & BACKYARD SCIENCE

Go somewhere and draw what you see! Look for animals!

If you can't go very far, go to a park or your own backyard.

Today's Date: _____

Today I Saw: _____

_____

_____

Today's Date:

TO-DO LIST

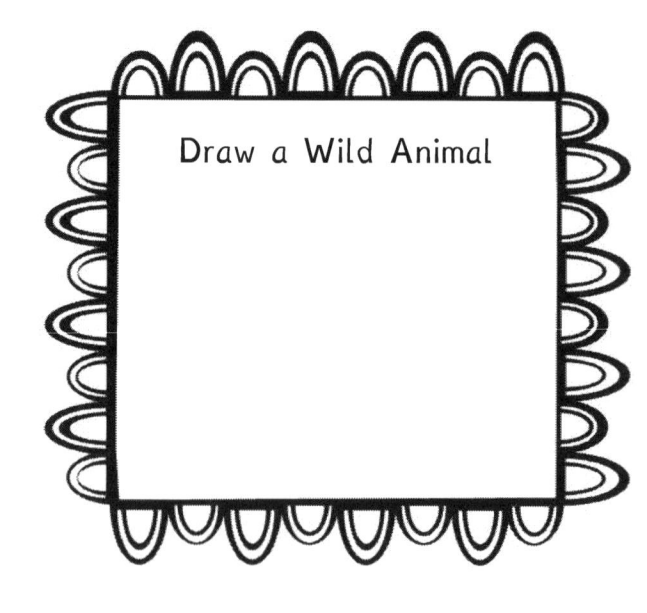

1._____
2._____
3._____
4._____

Draw a Wild Animal

How are you FEELING TODAY?

Draw a Pet

ANIMAL QUIZ

I am _____

I live in _____

I like to eat _____

My enemies are _____

Today's Date:
_____

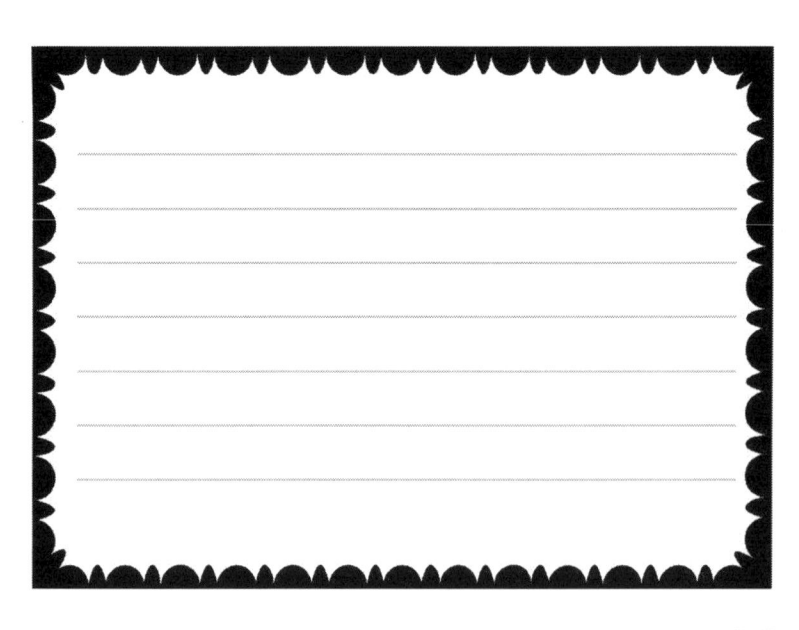

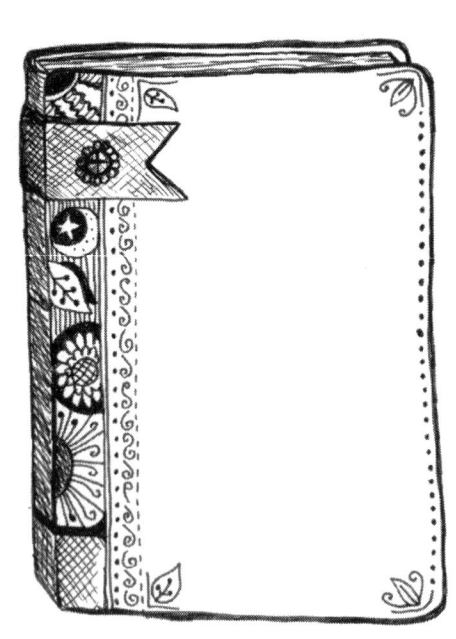

READING TIME

Write and draw about what you are reading.

FIELD TRIPS & BACKYARD SCIENCE

Go somewhere and draw what you see! Look for animals!

If you can't go very far, go to a park or your own backyard.

Today's Date: _____

Today I Saw: _____

_____

_____

_____

SPELLING TIME

Choose an Animal

_____

Look in your books for 10 words that have some of the same letters as this animal.

1. _____
2. _____
3. _____
4. _____
5. _____
6. _____
7. _____
8. _____
9. _____
10. _____

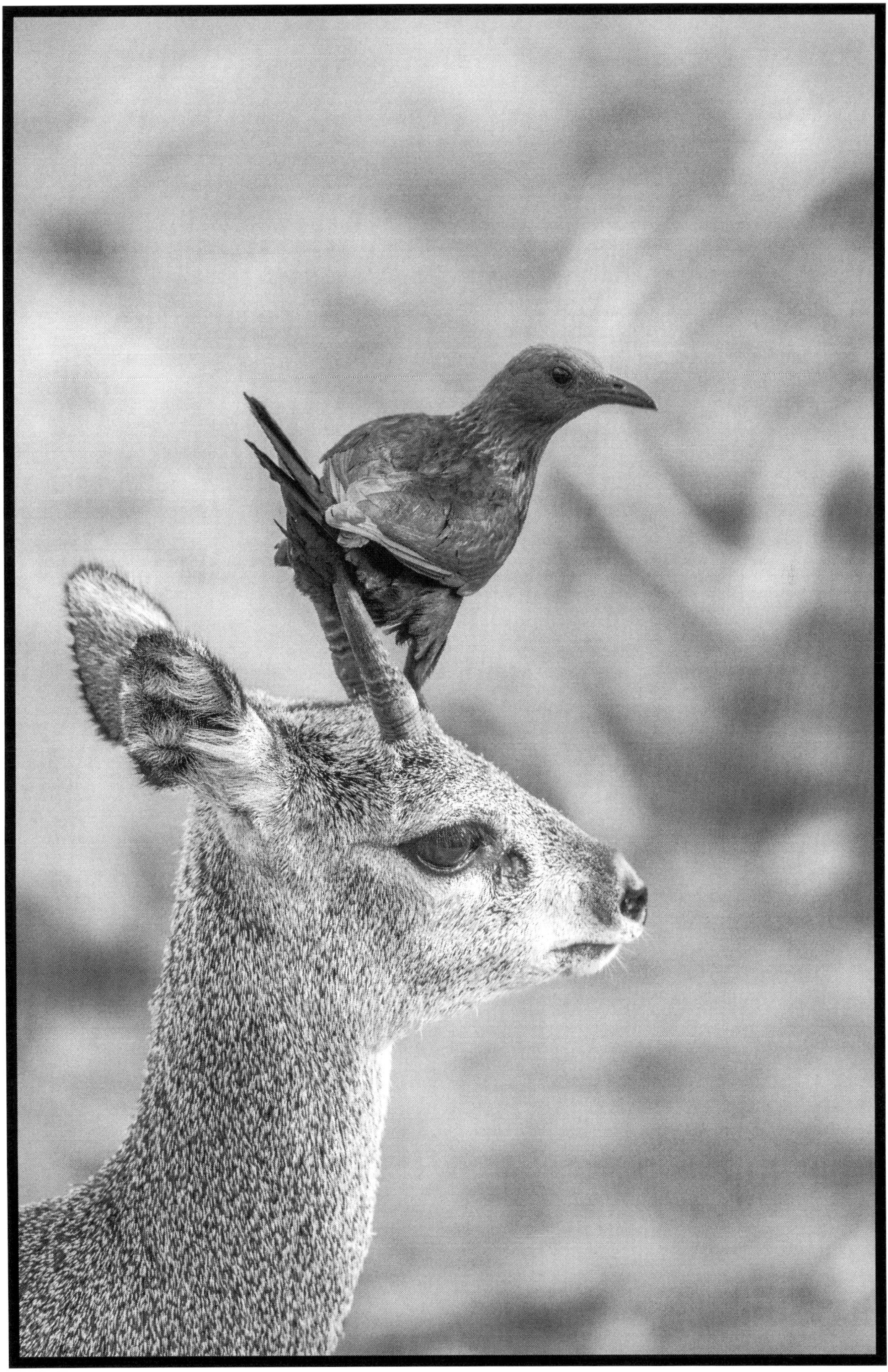

MOVIE TIME

Watch a movie or documentary about animals.

TITLE:_____

RATING

Draw Your Favorite Scenes:

DRAW MY HABITAT

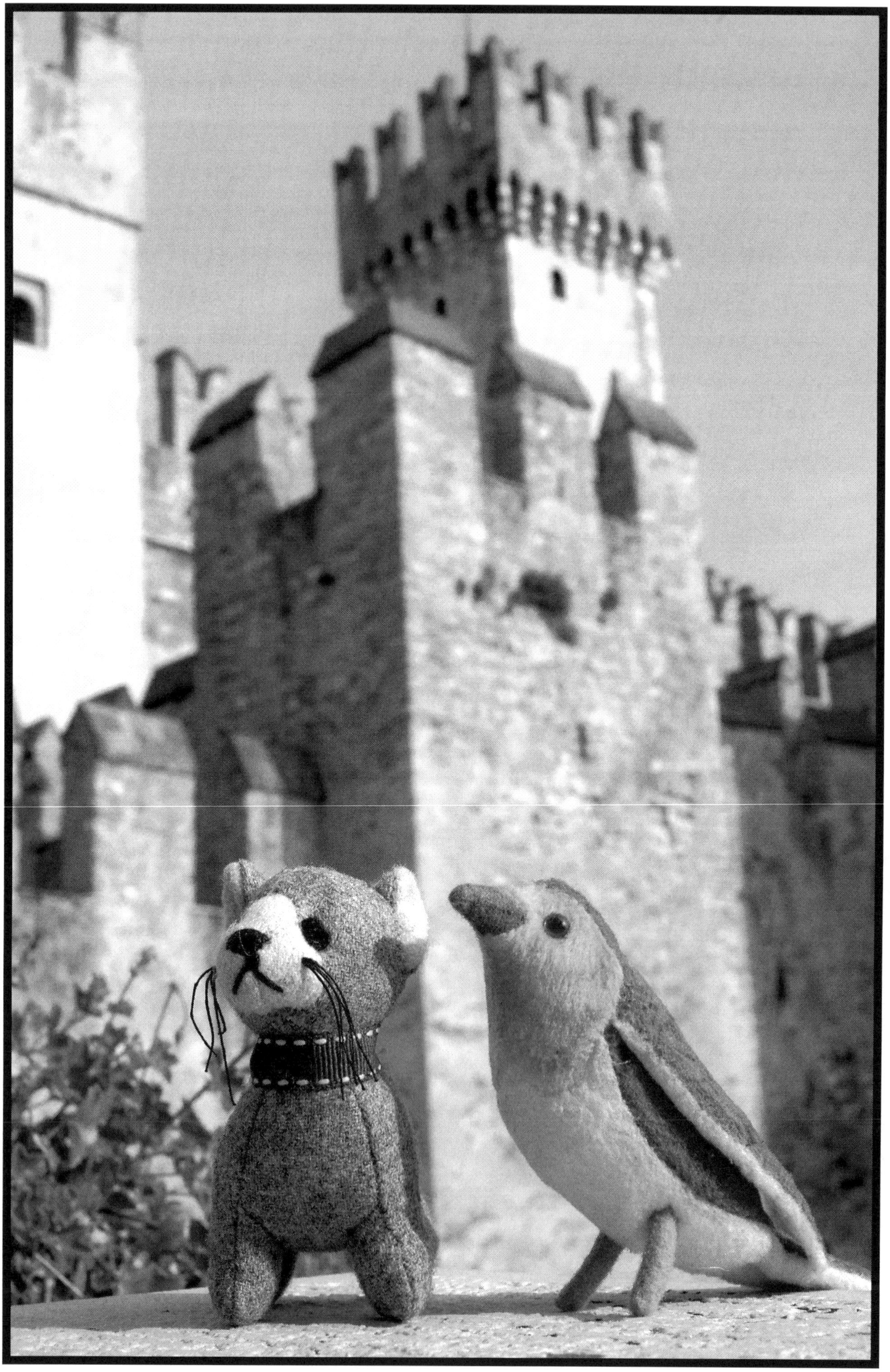

STORY WRITING TIME

If you can't think and write at the same time, record your story or ask someone older for help.

Title:

_____

Names & Descriptions of Characters:

_____
_____
_____
_____
_____

Base your story on the picture to the left.

_____
_____
_____
_____
_____
_____
_____
_____
_____
_____
_____
_____
_____
_____
_____
_____
_____
_____

SPELLING TIME

Choose a Letter: ___

Find 15 words that begin or end with that letter.

Five Nouns:

Write a silly story, poem, song or play using words from your spelling list.

Five Adjectives:

Three Animals:

Two Verbs:

CREATE A COMIC STRIP

Use your spelling words.

WHAT DID YOU LEARN ABOUT HISTORY TODAY?

WHAT DID YOU LEARN ABOUT SCIENCE TODAY?

WILDLIFE & GEOGRAPHY

RESEARCH AN ANIMAL OF YOUR CHOICE: _____

WHERE IN THE WORLD DOES THIS ANIMAL LIVE?

FUN FACTS:

DRAW THE ANIMAL:

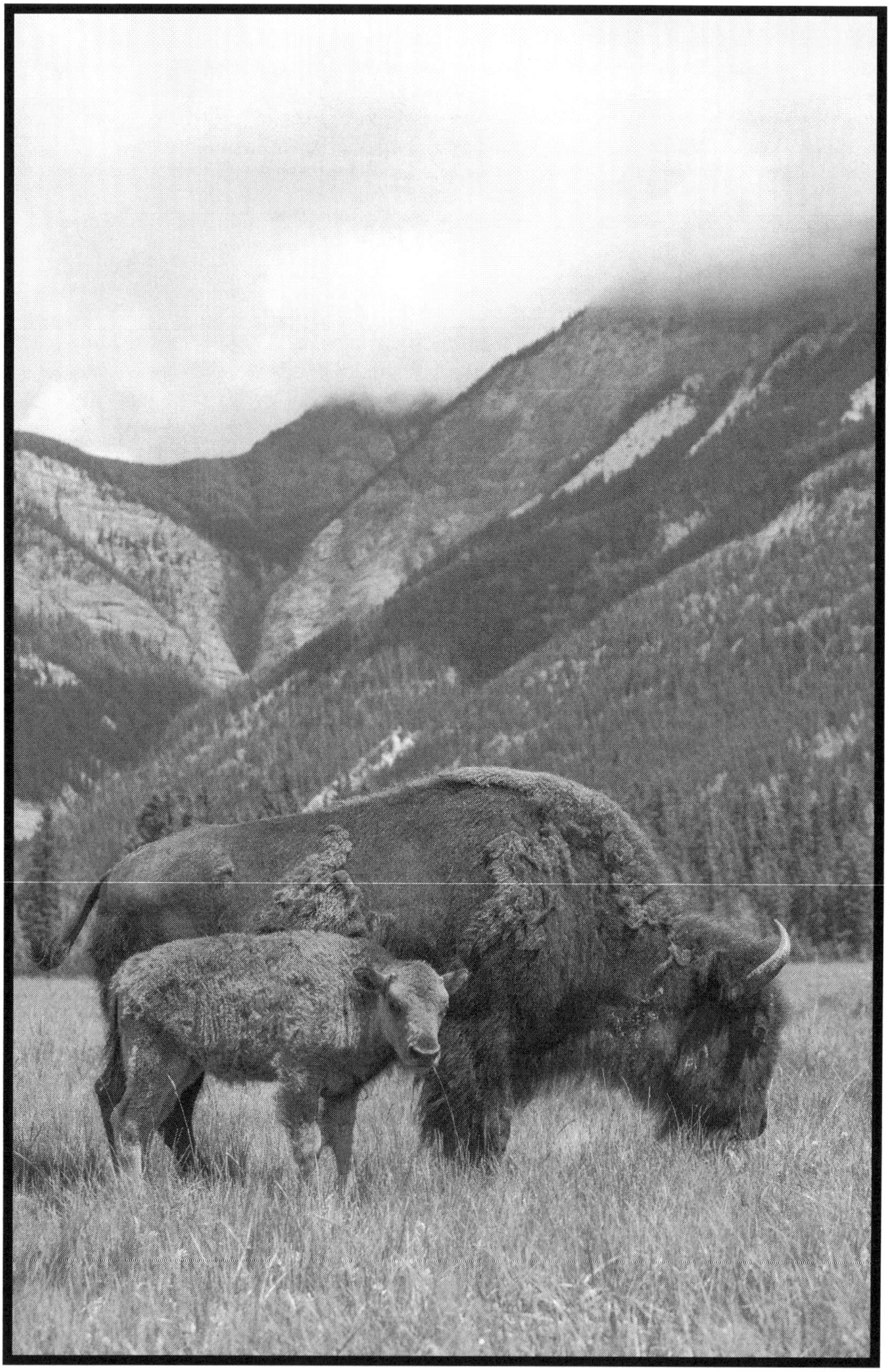

Trace & Color

Today's Date:

TO-DO LIST

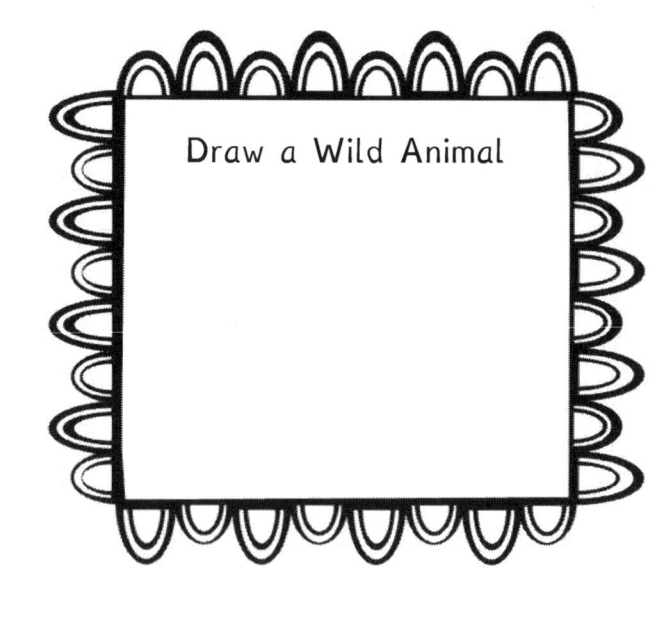

1._____
2._____
3._____
4._____

Draw a Wild Animal

How are you FEELING TODAY?

Draw a Pet

FIELD TRIPS & BACKYARD SCIENCE

Go somewhere and draw what you see! Look for animals!

If you can't go very far, go to a park or your own backyard.

Today's Date: _____

Today I Saw: _____
_____
_____
_____

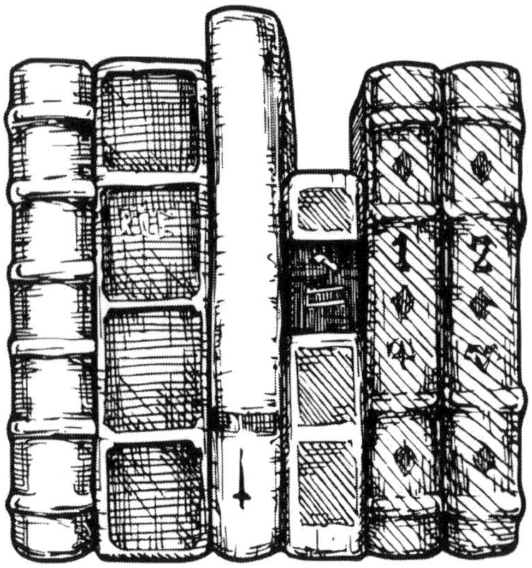

Today's Date:
_____

READING TIME

Write and draw about what you are reading.

COPYWORK

Copy a paragraph from one of your library books.

TITLE: _____ Page#_____

DRAWING TIME

Copy an illustration from one of your books.

ANIMAL QUIZ

I am _____

I live in _____

I like to eat _____

My enemies are _____

CURSIVE WRITING PRACTICE

A B C D E F G
H I J K L M
N O P Q R S T
U V W X Y Z

a b c d e f g h
i j k l m n o p
q r s t u v w x
y z 1 2 3 4 5 6 7 8 9 0

ORIGAMI CHALLENGE
CAN YOU MAKE THIS ANIMAL?

Set a timer.

Minutes:_____   Seconds:_____

A Pelican

LISTENING TIME

CLASSICAL MUSIC & LITERATURE

Today's Date:_____

Listen to an audio book or classical music.

Draw and doodle below.

I am listening to: _____

Today's Date:

TO-DO LIST

1._____

2._____

3._____

4._____

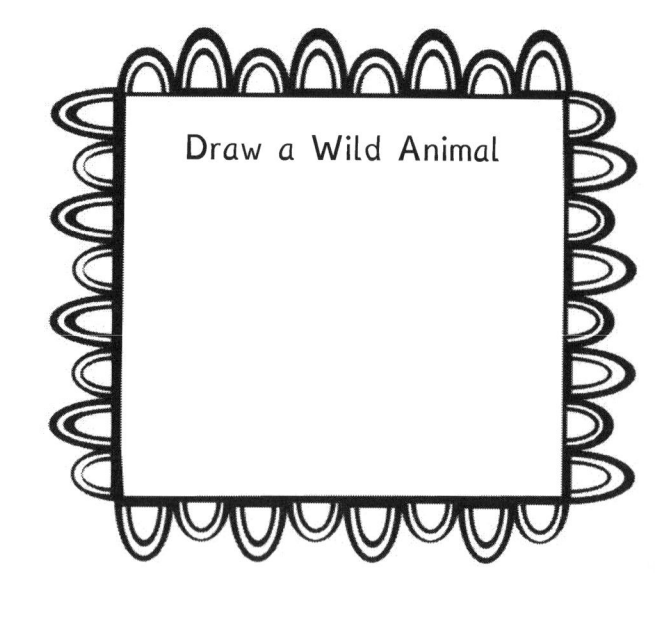

Draw a Wild Animal

How are you FEELING TODAY?

Draw a Pet

CREATIVE WRITING

Write a short story about this picture. Ask someone older to help you write the words.

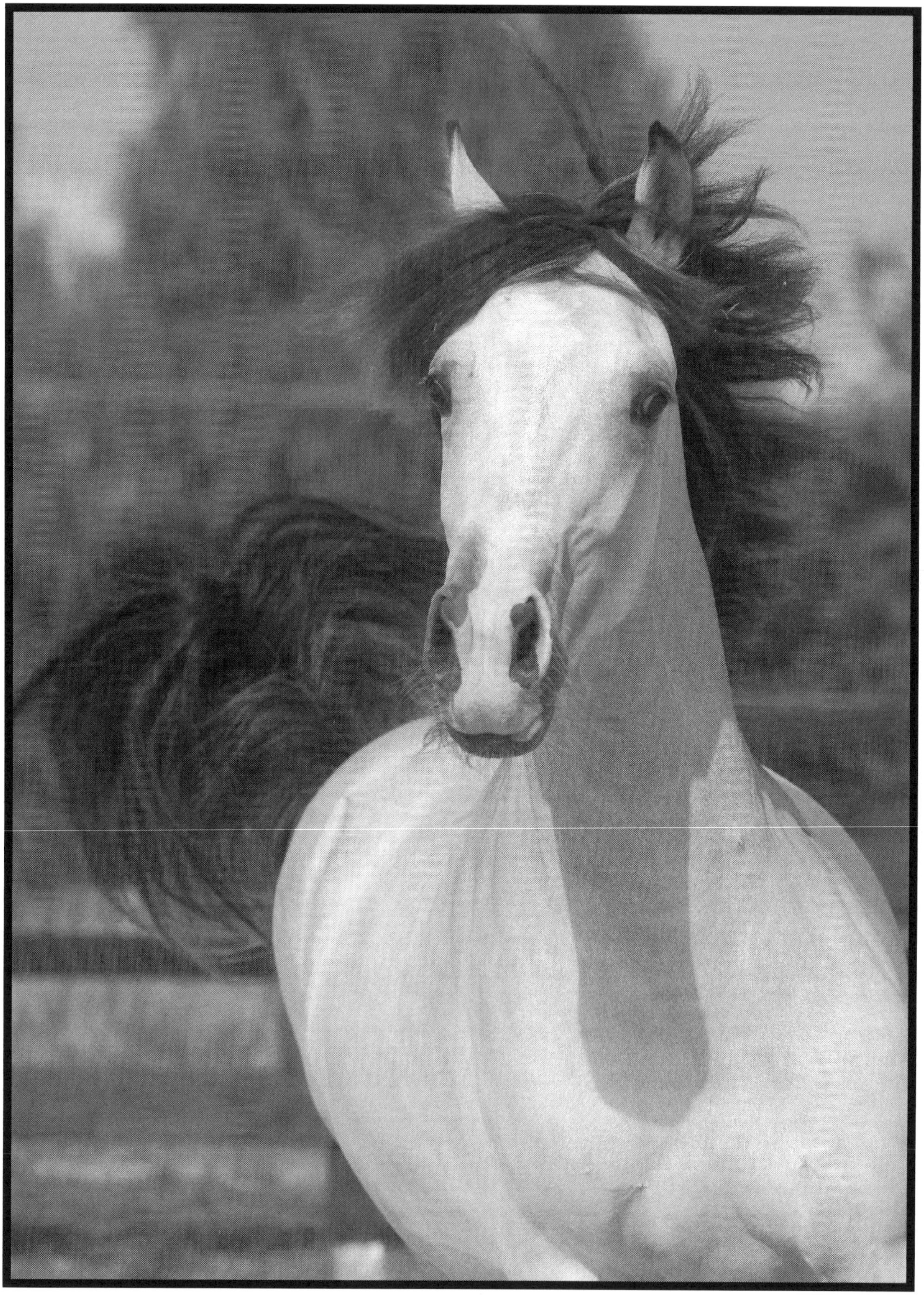

Trace & Color

Today's Date:

READING TIME

Write and draw about what you are reading.

FIELD TRIPS & BACKYARD SCIENCE

Go somewhere and draw what you see! Look for animals!

If you can't go very far, go to a park or your own backyard.

Today's Date: _____

Today I Saw: _____

_____

_____

SPELLING TIME

Choose a Letter: ___

Find 15 words that begin or end with that letter.

Five Nouns:

_____
_____
_____
_____
_____

Five Adjectives:

_____
_____
_____
_____
_____

Three Animals:

_____
_____
_____

Two Verbs:

_____
_____

Write a silly story, poem, song or play using words from your spelling list.

_____
_____
_____
_____
_____
_____
_____
_____
_____
_____
_____
_____
_____
_____
_____
_____
_____
_____

CREATE A COMIC STRIP

Use your spelling words.

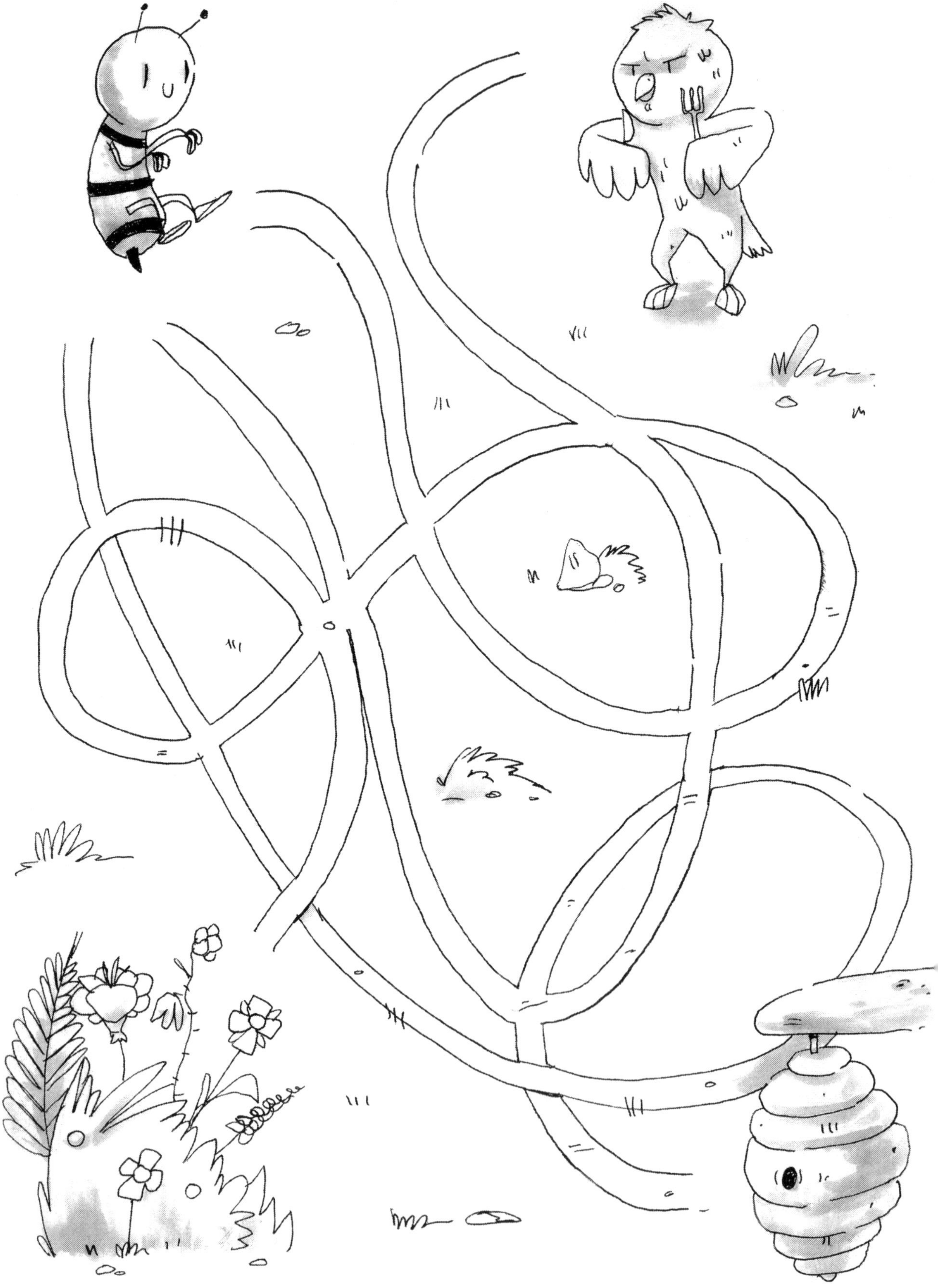

DRAW MY HABITAT

WHAT DID YOU LEARN ABOUT HISTORY TODAY?

WHAT DID YOU LEARN ABOUT SCIENCE TODAY?

WILDLIFE & GEOGRAPHY

RESEARCH AN ANIMAL OF YOUR CHOICE: _____

WHERE IN THE WORLD DOES THIS ANIMAL LIVE?

FUN FACTS:

DRAW THE ANIMAL:

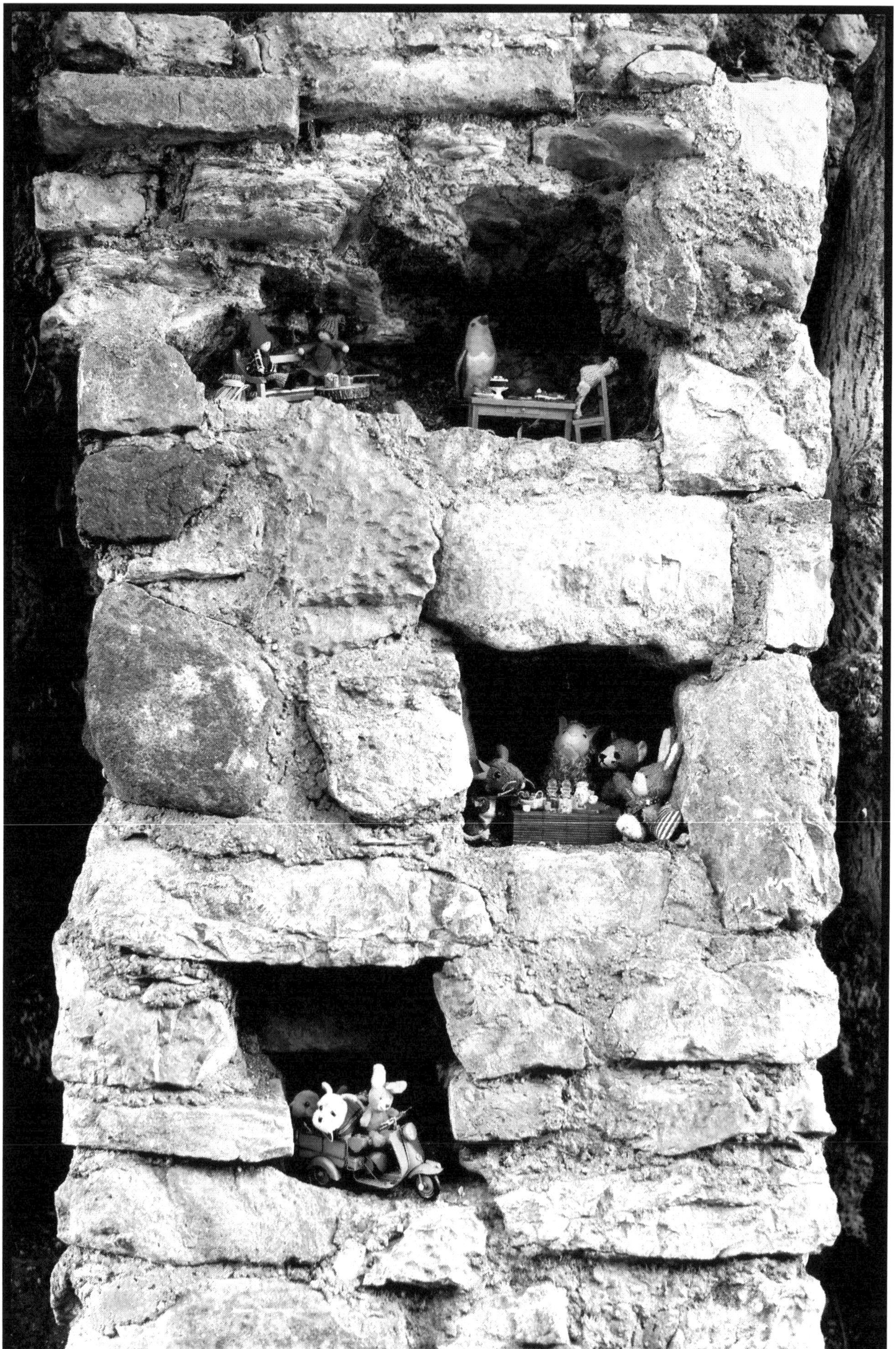

STORY WRITING TIME

If you can't think and write at the same time, record your story or ask someone older for help.

Title:

Names & Descriptions of Characters:

Base your story on the picture to the left.

MOVIE TIME

Watch a movie or documentary about animals.

TITLE:_____

Draw Your Favorite Scenes:

RATING

MATH & DESIGN TIME

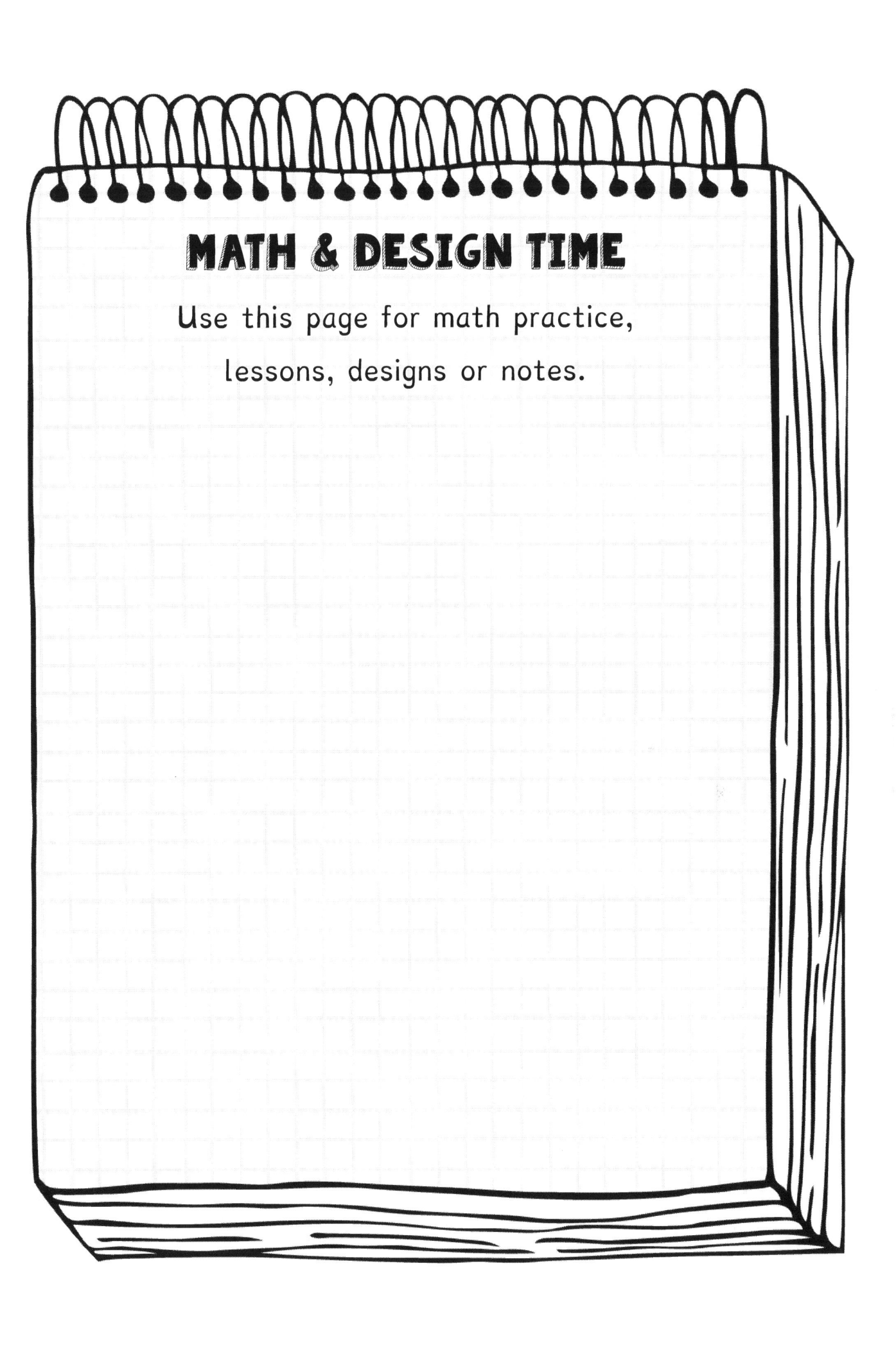

Use this page for math practice, lessons, designs or notes.

Today's Date:

TO-DO LIST

1._____

2._____

3._____

4._____

ABCDEFG
HIJKLMN
OPQRSTU
VWXYZ

How are you FEELING TODAY?

Draw a Pet

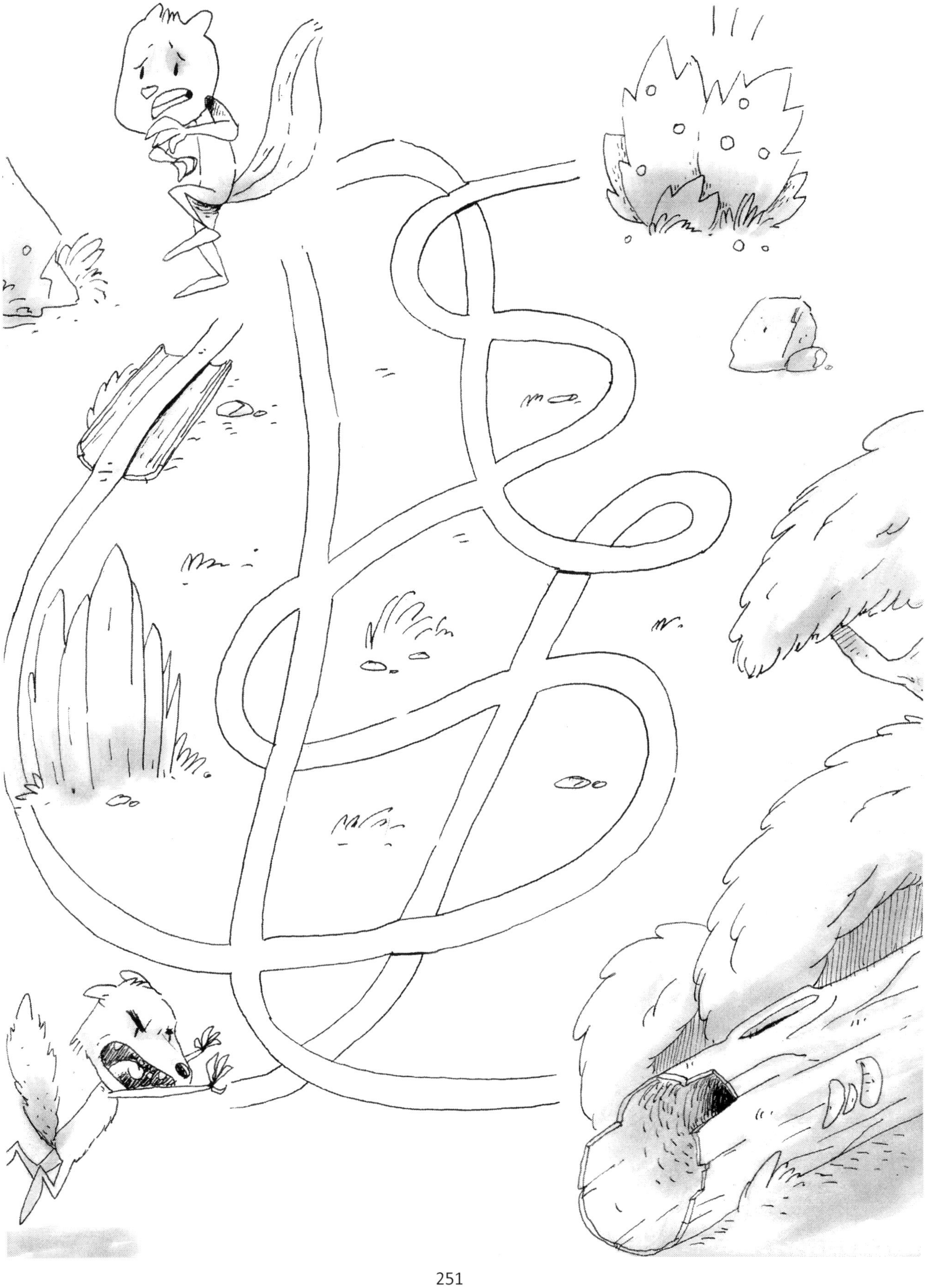

Today's Date:
_____

READING TIME

Write and draw about what you are reading.

FIELD TRIPS & BACKYARD SCIENCE

Go somewhere and draw what you see! Look for animals!

If you can't go very far, go to a park or your own backyard.

Today's Date: _____

Today I Saw: _____

_____

_____

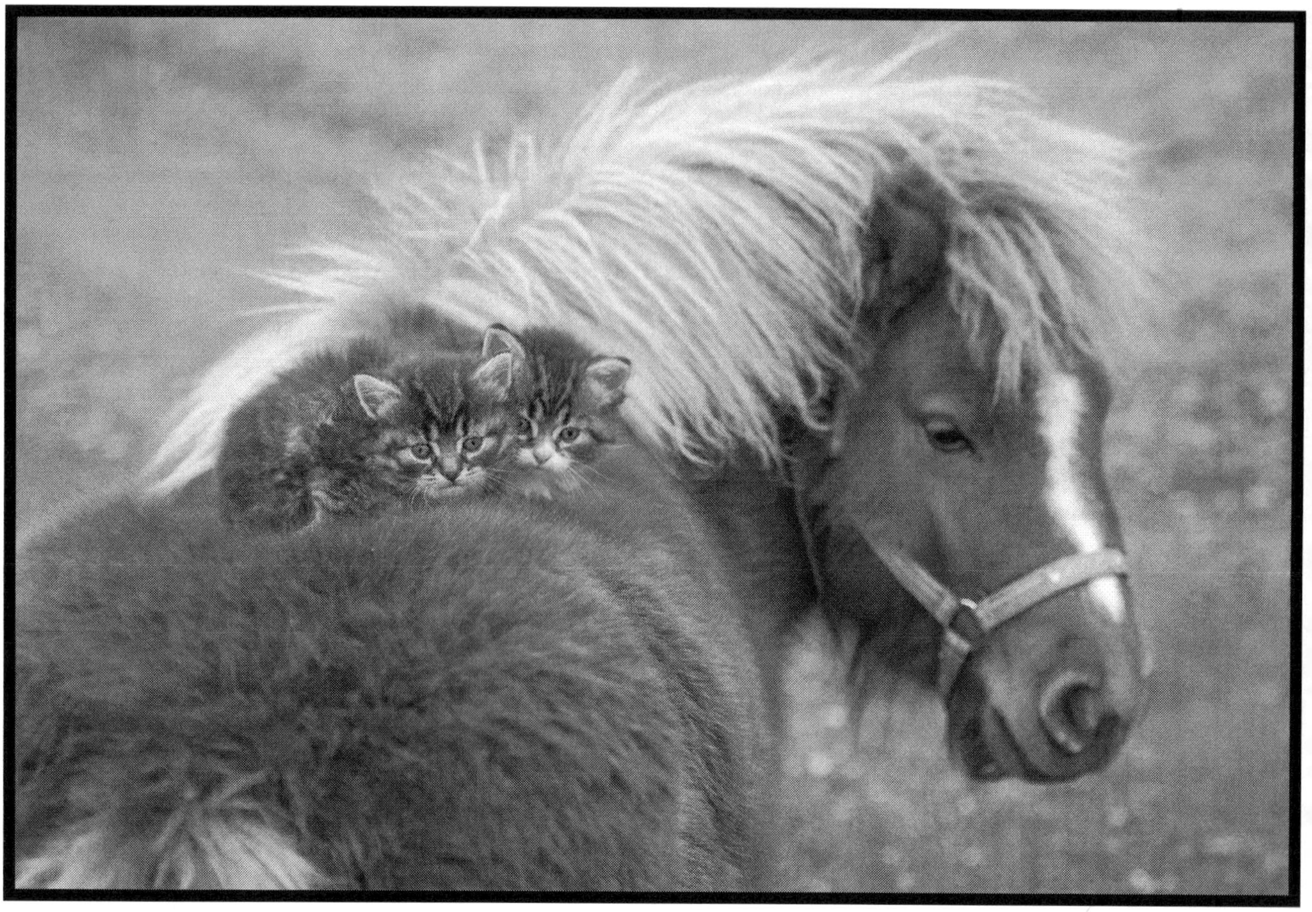

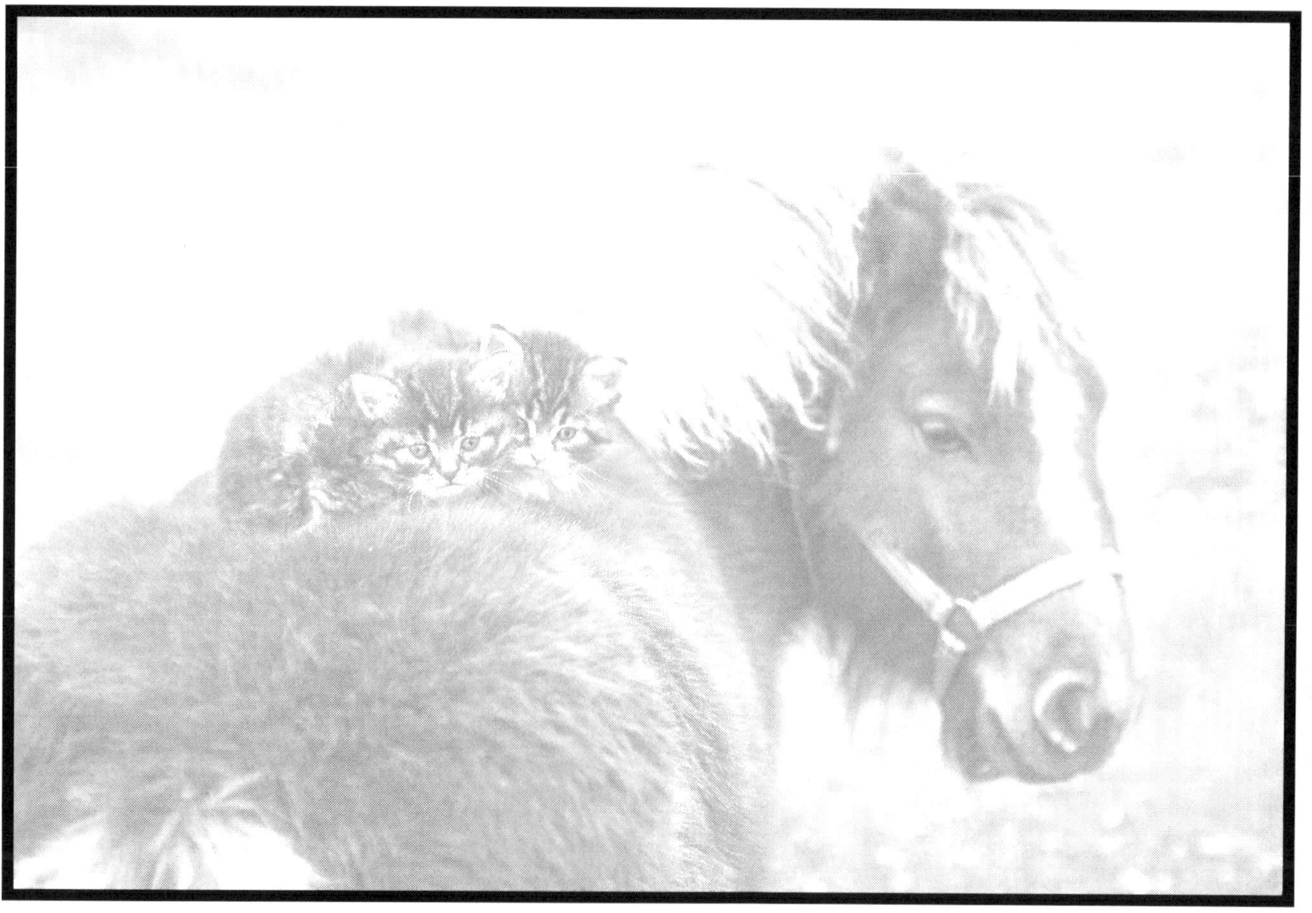

CURSIVE WRITING PRACTICE

A B C D E F G
H I J K L M
N O P Q R S T
U V W X Y Z

a b c d e f g h
i j k l m n o p
q r s t u v w x
y z 1 2 3 4 5 6 7 8 9 0

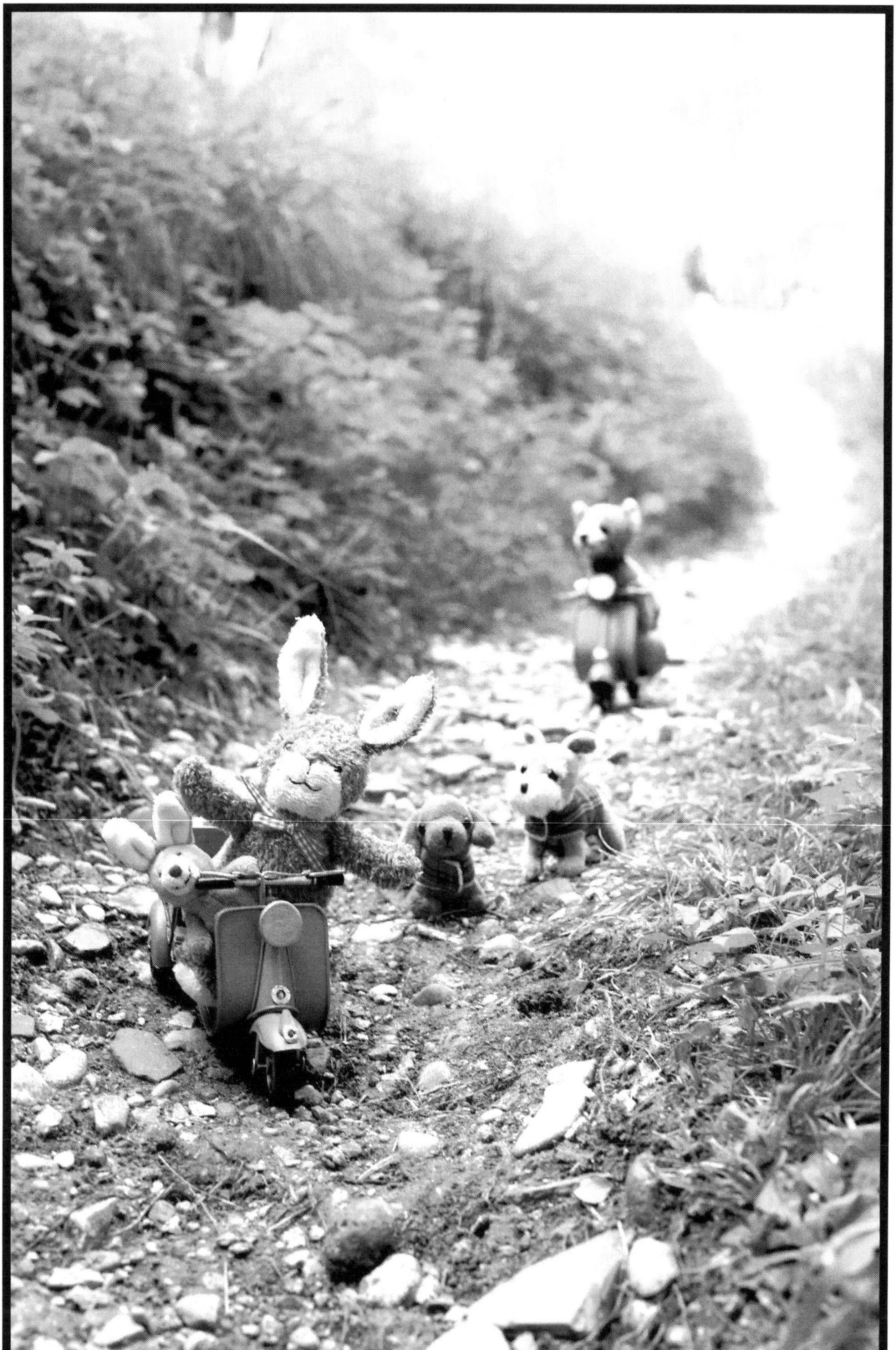

STORY WRITING TIME

If you can't think and write at the same time, record your story or ask someone older for help.

Title:

_____

Names & Descriptions of Characters:

_____
_____
_____
_____
_____

Base your story on the picture to the left.

_____
_____
_____
_____
_____
_____
_____
_____
_____
_____
_____
_____
_____
_____
_____
_____
_____
_____

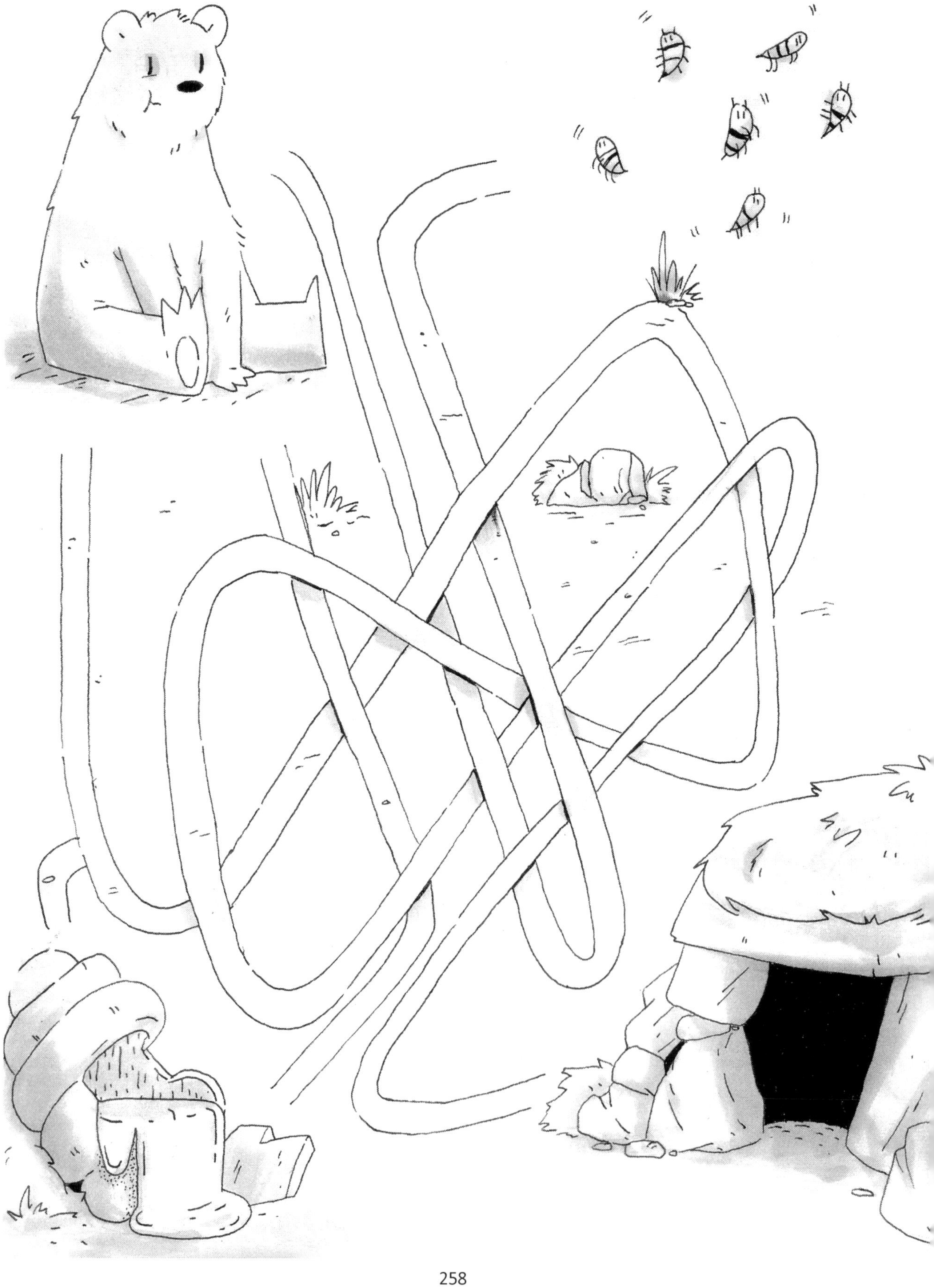

LISTENING TIME

CLASSICAL MUSIC & LITERATURE

Today's Date:_____

Listen to an audio book or classical music.

Draw and doodle below.

I am listening to: _____

SPELLING TIME

Choose a Letter: ___

Find 15 words that begin or end with that letter.

Five Nouns:

_____
_____
_____
_____
_____

Five Adjectives:

_____
_____
_____
_____
_____

Three Animals:

_____
_____
_____

Two Verbs:

_____
_____

Write a silly story, poem, song or play using words from your spelling list.

_____
_____
_____
_____
_____
_____
_____
_____
_____
_____
_____
_____
_____
_____
_____
_____

CREATE A COMIC STRIP

Use your spelling words.

WHAT DID YOU LEARN ABOUT HISTORY TODAY?

WHAT DID YOU LEARN ABOUT SCIENCE TODAY?

WILDLIFE & GEOGRAPHY

RESEARCH AN ANIMAL OF YOUR CHOICE: _____

WHERE IN THE WORLD DOES THIS ANIMAL LIVE?

FUN FACTS:

DRAW THE ANIMAL:

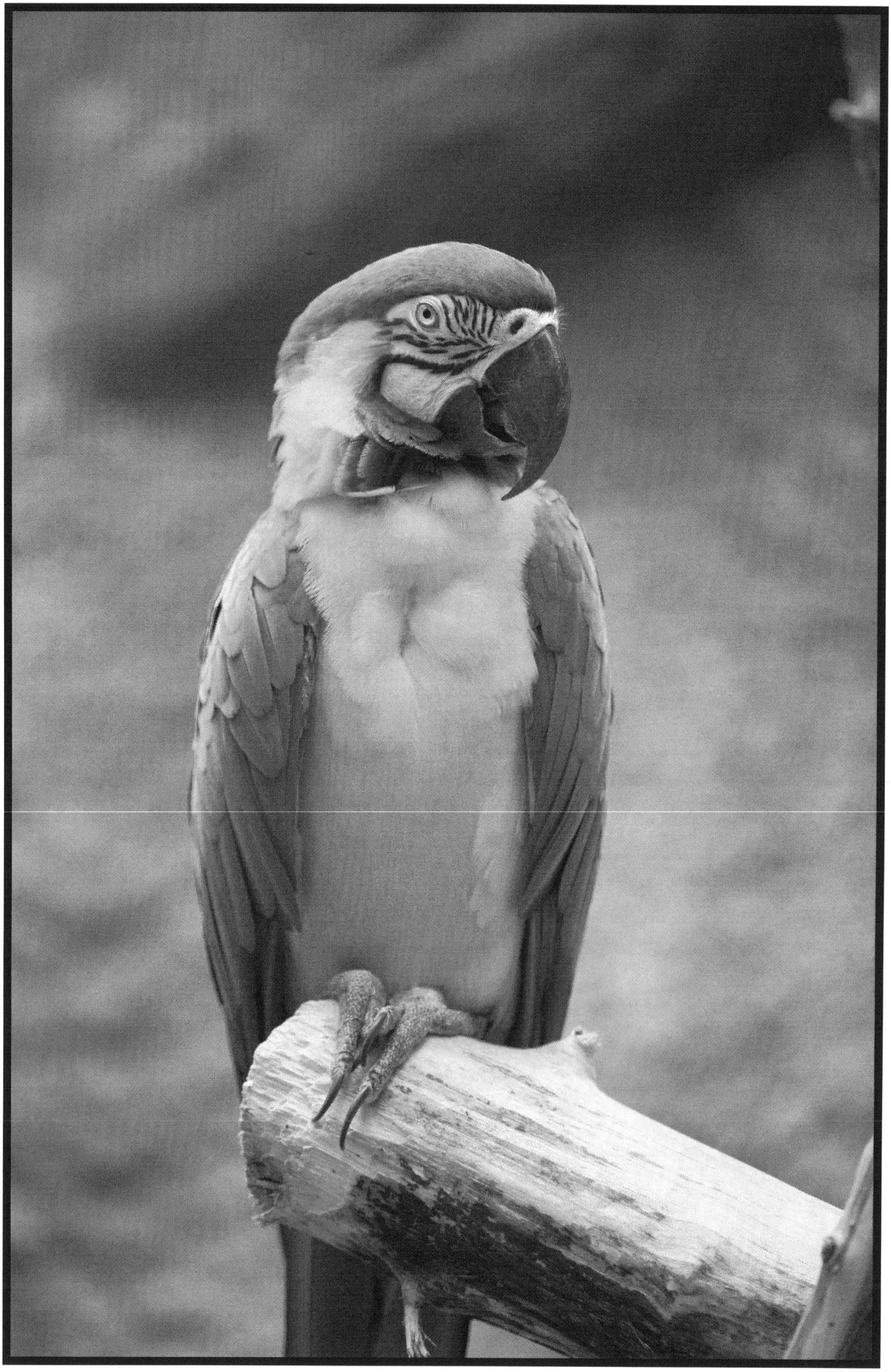

ORIGAMI CHALLENGE
CAN YOU MAKE THIS ANIMAL?

Set a timer.

Minutes:_____   Seconds:_____

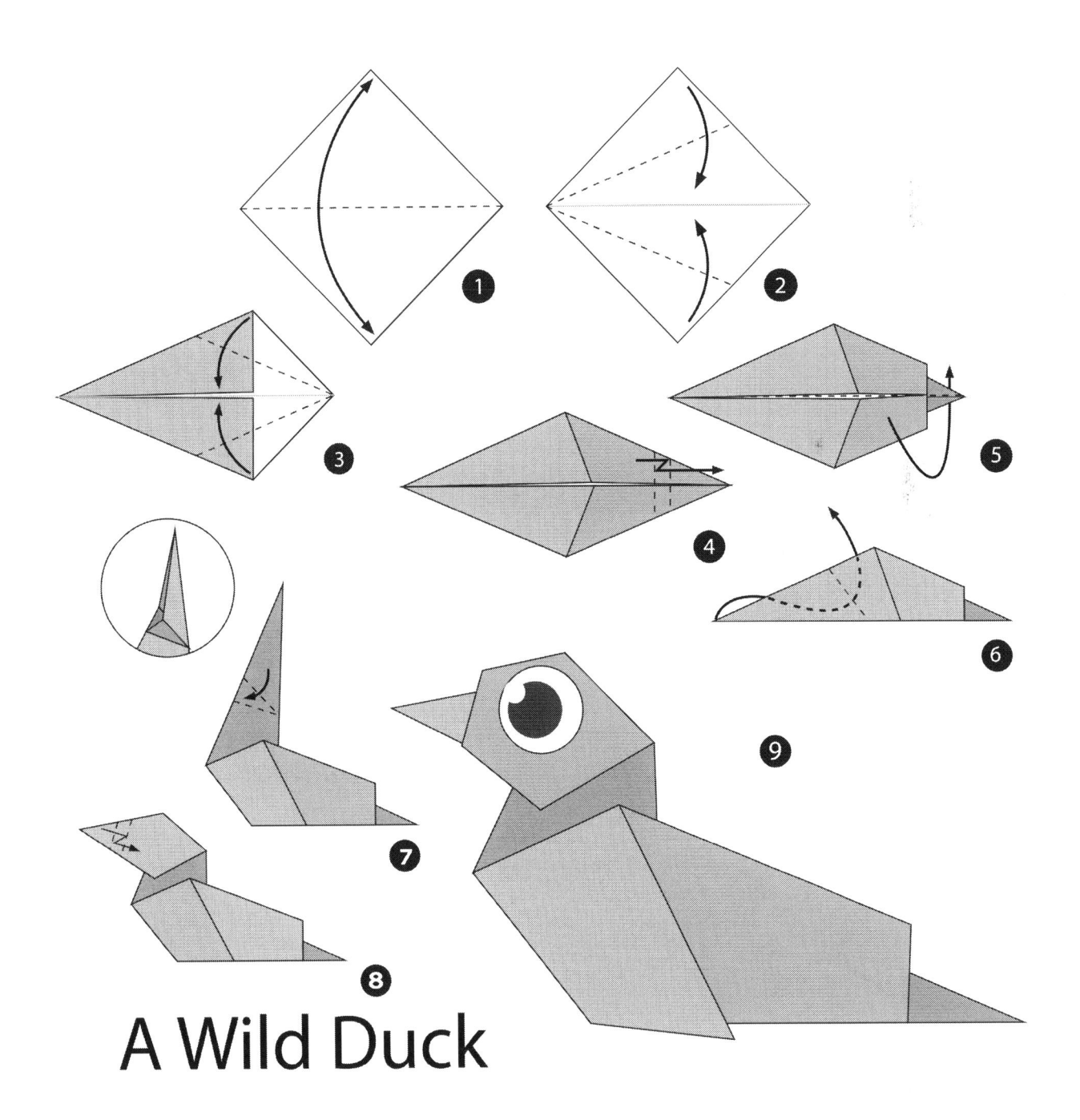

A Wild Duck

EXTRA BOOKS

1. Write down the titles on each cover below.

2. Keep your stack of books in a safe place so you can read a few pages from your books daily.

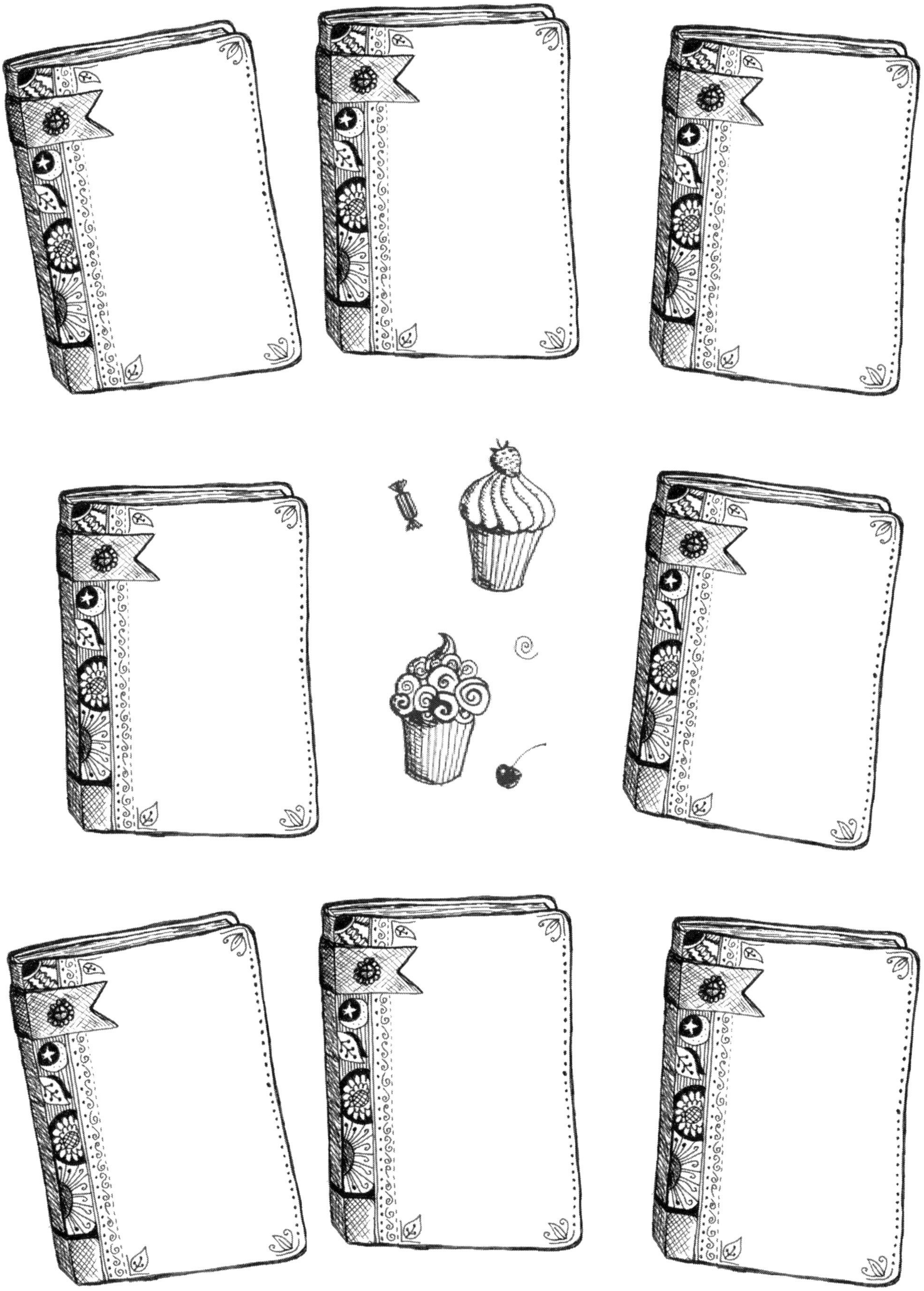

EXTRA BOOKS

1. Write down the titles on each cover below.

2. Keep your stack of books in a safe place so you can read a few pages from your books daily.

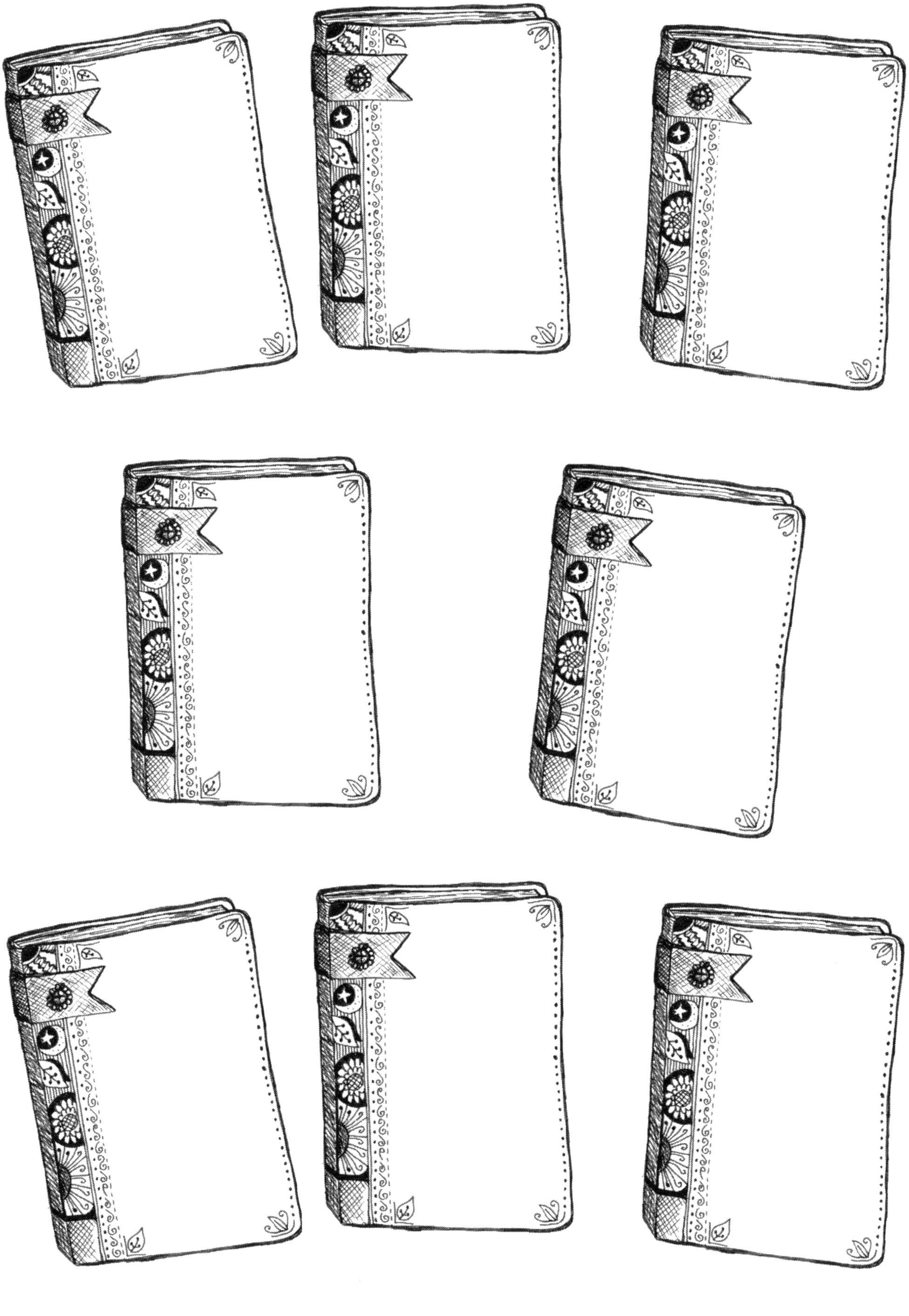

Do It Yourself HOMESCHOOL JOURNALS

Copyright Information

Do It YOURSELF Homeschool journal, and electronic printable downloads are for Home and Family use only. You may make copies of these materials for only the children in your household. All other uses of this material must be permitted in writing by the Thinking Tree LLC. It is a violation of copyright law to distribute the electronic files or make copies for your friends, associates or students without our permission.

Contact Us:

The Thinking Tree LLC

317.622.8852 PHONE (Dial +1 outside of the USA) 267.712.7889 FAX

FunSchoolingBooks.com

Made in United States
Orlando, FL
30 July 2024